338171 T. E.
(Lawrence of Arabia)

by

VICTORIA OCAMPO

Translated by

DAVID GARNETT

NEW YORK
E. P. DUTTON & CO., INC.

B
Lawrence

To
ROGER CAILLOIS

With whom, on a road in France, some-where between Paris and Rheims, I talked for the first time about *Seven Pillars of Wisdom*. Because he encouraged me to write these pages which are a slight indica-tion of an admiration which he shares and of which he was the principal confidant and the best interpreter.

13 November 1942

TRANSLATOR'S NOTE

338171 T. E. was written by Victoria Ocampo in French in 1942. The present translation is of that book but has the additional notes of the Spanish translation published in 1963, together with an introduction by A. W. Lawrence.

I have put Señora Ocampo's numerous quotations from *Seven Pillars of Wisdom* back into T. E. Lawrence's own words and wish to express my grateful acknowledgments to *Doubleday & Co. Inc.*, and to the Lawrence Trustees for permission to do so.

David Garnett

He asked us to call him T. E., because he said that was the only part of his name which really belonged to him, and people who were fond of him should call him that.

Florence Doubleday
T. E. Lawrence by his Friends

CONTENTS

INTRODUCTION

Because of her interest in my brother, Victoria Ocampo sought me out at Cambridge in 1946, and at that first meeting she gave me a copy of her book, *338171 T. E.*, of which I had not heard, since she had published it in Buenos Aires during the war. I started to read it with some reluctance, remembering how derivative and, at the best, superficial I had considered the studies of him written on the European continent, while the more ambitious of them had, in my judgment, wrongly interpreted the character they attempted to portray. This woman, from another end of the world, had presumably been confronted by far greater barriers to understanding the man she never met, whose problems arose in physical and spiritual environments necessarily unfamiliar to her, and from circumstances which must seem no less strange than the events of remote centuries.

I found that she had passed through the barriers as though they formed no obstacle, and that her book gave the most profound and the best-balanced of all portraits of my brother; I had, and still have, no doubt of its accuracy (and I knew him, I think, quite well). Other books have since been published, and there are some which utilised personal knowledge of him, but hers retains its pre-eminence, and fresh evidence has in no way affected its validity.

Astonishing as her achievement appeared upon slight acquaintance with her, it grew to the proportions of a miracle when I came to realise how utterly different from his her life and ways had always been. Not one comparable experience or condition had they ever shared, so far as I could learn, while they stood at contrary poles in their manner of thought and action, and even in their inclinations. Their principles, their whole philosophy, conflicted in almost every respect. His had been moulded by influences from beyond her horizon— biblical protestantism, ancient Greece, the Middle Ages, Arabia; from all these he selected substance with which to build his religion of austerity. She, indeed, had witnessed something akin to its basis, for, as she herself recognised, there is an affinity between the pampa and the desert, between gauchos and bedouin, but the infection barely touched her, if at all; that she had not proved altogether immune may be suspected because of her imaginative sympathy with those, such as Gandhi and Teresa of Avila, who rejected material possessions. Hence, too, she may have been ready to applaud, as a spectator, T. E. L.'s brutal rejection of the style of living which she demanded for her own. But she was positively antipathetic to most of his interests. Even as regards the arts, where they might have had common ground, their tastes rarely coincided; both of them flamed with an idolatrous devotion to books, but not to the same books. And there seemed no other obvious points of resemblance between the two of them except their passion for freedom, with its concomitants (notably a boundless generosity), and the fact that nature had endowed each with a supernormal vigour and forcefulness.

Yet this dead man exerted an obsessive fascination upon her. It had induced her not merely to read but to memorise everything relevant to understanding him, and she fitted together all the fragmentary information with the accuracy of a computing machine. In addition, she brought to this work a special type of human insight, one which is invariably the gift of a particular emotion. Though she saw, with equal clarity, his virtues and his faults, his successes and his failings, his wisdom and his silliness, the completeness of her vision did not in the least reduce his attraction for her. In fact, she loved him. That inexplicable phenomenon explains the uncanny truthfulness of her interpretation.

A. W. Lawrence

A MAN OF THE DESERT

> We were a self-centred army without parade or gesture,
> devoted to freedom, the second of man's creeds, a purpose
> so ravenous that it devoured all our strength, a hope so
> transcendent that our earlier ambitions faded in its glare.
> *Seven Pillars of Wisdom*. Ch. I

SOME REGIONS OF the earth, which are not rich or picturesque, attract us because of a mysterious relationship we have with them. Their character and size seem to be the image of some secret landscape which we see with the inner eye when we are blind to our actual surroundings. And sometimes these twin images—the real and the ideal—coincide so closely that we can no longer tell which of the two is a copy of the other.

The great plains—the pampas of my home—can only be loved by those who feel in them:

> The pleasure of believing all we see
> Is boundless, as we wish our souls to be.

T. E. Lawrence loved the desert in that way. It had won him by its vastness and its suggestion of infinity. As a young man he had quoted those lines of Shelley to explain his feeling for it. I put this first of all because like most such preferences, it is a revealing one. It is a clue which must not be forgotten when we try to thread the labyrinth in which Lawrence himself often nearly lost his way. It is by such preferences, such signs, that the living and the dead make themselves known to us, so that we can tell what they are like, where they will lead us and in what hidden corner of their consciousness they store their purest treasures. But these signs are in cipher. One can only understand their meaning when one knows the code by heart. The preferences which one shares with another person are the most favourable ground on which to meet him. A. W. Lawrence realised that when he undertook the difficult task of revealing to the public all the multiple facets of his brother's genius. To achieve this he asked all those who had known that inconsistent man to write a few pages about him, keeping strictly to that aspect of his personality which had struck them the most, or with which they had had most personal contact, or affinity. The idea was excellent as is proved by the resulting book. Colonel Lawrence's mother tells us about a child—her own. Then there are his schoolfellows and fellow students at the University, those with whom he worked as an archaeologist, those with whom he served during the war; those with whom he talked of literature and music, his feelings about books and politics and speed-boats. Each of the contributors had known his own Lawrence—from Allenby and Wavell, his commanders, to Bernard Shaw, David Garnett, Winston Churchill, Jonathan Cape, Forster, Lord Halifax and many others.

I nurse a hope of one day editing a supplement to that book with the collaboration of a group of those who (like myself) have become Lawrence's friends since his death; friends whom he has made by what he left of himself in *Seven Pillars of Wisdom* and in his letters. These pages are only a preparation for this project—preliminary material for a work which can only come into existence with the spiritual co-operation of a number of people.

One day when I was having lunch at a big embassy I discovered by chance that my neighbour at the table had known Colonel Lawrence in Egypt. My pleasure and my expectations were soon dashed—for the Englishman (who was quite free of any malice) could only give me a vague colourless description of him. Moreover he did not think him very illustrious. In his eyes Lawrence was a soldier who like many others had rendered services to his country and a writer, who, like many others, had written a description of the war. I did not press the subject for I saw that I was dealing with a man devoid of imaginative understanding. But this experience consoled me a little for having been Lawrence's contemporary without ever having seen him. For I had just had proof that some people had had the misfortune of seeing him without ever having known what he was like. Could I reasonably complain

of being one of those who had known what he was like
without ever having set eyes on him?

I have met him in the books and in the music which
he loved. But above all I have met him in the plains of
the pampas, in those plains where he sought alternately
to lose himself and to discover his own nature and
which was for him, from early years, the desert: "The
desert whose daily sparseness gave value to every man."

In those vast unrelieved spaces the centre of things
follows us, it moves with us no matter in which direction we set out. We cannot escape it. It is always where
we are; it is involved in us, falling so exactly on our
heads that it vanishes and has no existence apart from
us, so that it is like our noonday shadow. We are ourselves the centre of all things. Yet it is as though at
midday we were only the shadow of a shadow; the
shadow of a nothing blotted out by the sun. Our very
movements seem wiped out, for the centre moves as we
move and the horizon remains in consequence for ever
equally far off. It encircles us and shows itself to us on
all sides tamely and with no apparent obstacle. It
shows itself thus and we despair of ever reaching it.
Yet we travel towards it always, well knowing that it is
beyond our reach, and giving no thought and not a
glance at nearer objectives. . . . We are doomed by this
centre within ourselves; we are chained to remain in
the same spot although it does not destroy our eager
efforts—to travel on and there is no visible range of

mountains to discourage us. Immensity surrounds us with an emptiness which is full of starting points: nothing is hidden. Not even the blue horizon which girdles the impassible earth with a circle of sky. And we are always there—the centre of the visible world, free to travel where we will in the solitude which engulfs us. Free. But free of what?

Dressed in white robes like an Arab, wearing a Meccan circlet of red and gold about his head and a golden dagger at his waist, steeped in the desert, T. E. Lawrence said one day to his men: "Failure seems God's freedom to mankind." Perhaps at the moment that he spoke he did not believe completely in the truth of his own words. Later on he must have repeated them to himself for his own triumph was a defeat for him and he believed he could find in defeat the only way of reaching, as though on tiptoe, the springs of liberty which honours, conquests and glory had threatened to dry up.

In giving a brief account of the history of this man I shall not attempt to describe the victorious commander or the fascinating writer. (It is for others to make a minute analysis of his battles and his prose.) I want particularly to trace the development of a moral conflict in him which grew and grew and was interrupted only by his death. Perhaps Lawrence's worst fault was in taking delight in too many acts of self-denial. But can one call what was evidently his *dharma*, the law of his inner being, a fault?

His soul was crippled like that of Arjuna* on the field of battle. Nothing could dissipate the anxiety which paralysed him. Like Arjuna, Lawrence no longer desired victory or power, or pleasure. He was a man of the wide spaces. And it was in those regions of the earth, peopled with nothing, that I got to know him.

* In the Baghavad-gita.

A CRITIC IN ACTION

CERTAIN MORAL QUALITIES are even more striking than the curved smile or the tone of voice which accentuates and accompanies them. These characteristics were so large a part of Lawrence that all his various friends were aware of them in the same way. All of them agree in stressing his passion for freedom, his hatred of injustice, his courage, his physical stamina and his moral integrity, his critical powers—analytic and descriptive as a writer—rapid of decision and lucid of mind as a leader during battle—his reserve, his personal asceticism, and his conscience as scrupulous as that of any man living. It would have been as difficult for them to differ on such points as about the colour of his eyes which were an unchanging blue, or about his build—short and slight.

Certain features appeared predominant to certain observers; for interpretations and slight differences arise with varying angles of view and lighting. There are even ill-natured interpretations and false details.*

* I did not foresee in 1941 when I wrote this book that malice could reach the height—that is sink to the depths—to which Richard Aldington carried it fourteen years later. Harold Nicolson, whom no one would call kind to Lawrence and who criticises him with evident antipathy, finished an article published in *The*

But these judgments can only come from a disinterested clear-minded critic. I have never believed in perspicacity springing from hatred, or wisdom springing from envy.

The author of *Seven Pillars of Wisdom*, "the uncrowned king of Arabia", did not escape detractors and hero worshippers. He was too conspicuous for that. But his real friends saw both his qualities and his faults, knew both his exploits and his blind spots, his genius and his limitations. It was Lawrence who had taught them to see them. For nobody spoke of his weaknesses more harshly than he did himself. He was simultaneously a man of action and an onlooker at his own life—no one more so. The onlooker was pitiless to the man of action, the latter cruel to the onlooker. If the actor made a gesture that was wrong, that was not faithful to the truth and suited to the occasion, the

---

Observer, 30 January 1955, in the following words : "T. E. was cursed with a neurotic and infinitely complicated character, and one which cannot be judged by conventional standards. Mr. Aldington is probably correct in attributing his retreat from his own personality, his plunge into the ranks, as due to some Calvinistic obsession with sin and atonement. Yet he treats as an eccentric, and almost comic, episode what was a symptom of deep spiritual crisis. Such agonies should be handled with respect. I am obliged to Mr. Aldington for having forced me to think more highly of T. E. Lawrence than I ever thought before." And in the same article Harold Nicolson said : "It is as if someone were to describe Shakespeare's atrocious table manners at the Mermaid tavern while omitting to mention that he also wrote plays."

onlooker heaped contempt on him. If the onlooker spoke out of turn, unaccompanied and unjustified, the actor laughed derisively and bitterly. Lawrence said in one of his letters: "We should not in thought pass the bounds we set ourselves in deed, or our ideas will not ring true." That was an obsession with him. One might perhaps have replied that few men can live up to their ideals and that it is better that they should have them. By thinking them over the green fruit may be brought to ripeness.

Lawrence would have despised himself too much if he had indulged in generous words while living a mean life, or have admired courage and proved a coward in face of danger, have professed a theoretical disgust of the flesh and have succumbed to carnal temptations. A voice nagged at him the whole time. It was not that of Lady Macbeth driving her husband to commit murder, but that of his own conscience forcing him to live up to his own principles.

> "Art thou afeared
> To be the same in thine own act and valour
> As thou art in desire?"*

The closely interwoven thoughts and actions of Colonel Lawrence seem, as I meditate upon them, to be a re-affirmation of the moral world in an age when to drift,

* *Macbeth* I, vii.

to be uncertain and cowardly, to be ready to gloss over one's own frailties and to be indulgent of one's own interests, to be divided and weakened by interior anarchy, contribute more than at any time to upset the balance of the world of right and wrong. But it is only in that world that the existence of men like Colonel Lawrence makes sense and that books like *Seven Pillars of Wisdom* have a value except as decorations.

In a letter to Edward Garnett Lawrence analysed a criticism of his work and said: "Read talks as though I had been making a book and not a flesh and blood revolt." He should have written: "Read talks as though I had been making only a book." For what is rare in him is that he has succeeded in doing both things. *Seven Pillars* has the indispensable elements of great literature: form and content. Lawrence might well have had things to say but if he had not been able to handle words with the ability with which he handled men, his book would never have begun to exist and as a work of art it would have ranked with those written by so many dictators. If he had been nothing but a handler of words with no other care or need except to construct phrases to astonish us, his book would have been some "forgotten booklet of sonorous inanity" like that of so many writers.

Writing the story of the Arab Revolt will make Lawrence live longer in men's minds than having fought through it in Arabia. Victories gained on the field of battle are often more perishable than those won in lonely rooms against invisible enemies.

The Englishman who with no malicious intention saw nothing in Lawrence but a soldier who had done his duty—though perhaps he had done rather better than others—was not completely wrong in one respect. Some other men—I say some—might possibly have endured what he endured, fought as he fought and have conquered as he did. But I don't know of one who at the same time would have succeeded in feeling as he felt, of thinking as he thought and of living as he lived and have written of the effects of his experiences in a style which at moments is Shakespearian. For Lawrence had that "gift of language" which often corrupts those who possess it so that it becomes in their hands not an indispensable instrument but an end in itself. To speak of *Seven Pillars of Wisdom* is to speak of its author for he was on the same plane as the book. That is what seems to me to make him such an exemplary figure. In him thought and action kept in step; there was style in the manner of his writing and the manner of his life, style in what he chose to do, just as in the words he chose to use.

It is not often that men with the gifts needed for material success are particularly scrupulous, or that great strategists are also experts in spiritual self-examination for any flaw. Lawrence was. He was an explorer of the desert and the explorer of his hidden ego, a destroying angel charging the Turks at the head of a band of Arabs and a destroying angel turning inwards upon himself. He fought with every ounce of his courage and cunning to take Damascus and then wrote: "We took Damascus and I feared. More than three arbitrary days would have quickened in me a root of authority."

It was a fear of dominating others lest he should be enslaved himself by a lust for power.

His passion for Arabia did not make Lawrence exceptional. He shared it with numbers of Englishmen whose names appear in the *Encyclopaedia Britannica* ... many in our own time. To begin with the women: there was Lady Hester Stanhope, Pitt's niece who lived in the desert like an Arab Sheikh, and Gertrude Bell, Lawrence's great friend. As for the men it is enough to mention Doughty whose celebrated book of his travels, *Arabia Deserta,* was Lawrence's bible.

If childhood leaves indelible marks on a man for the whole of his life and if the man to be can be discerned already in the child, as scientists assert, and as we believe ourselves when we analyse our own memories and inclinations, it is essential to study Lawrence's childhood before going on to *Seven Pillars of Wisdom* and the work and life of its author.

CHILDHOOD

CHILDHOOD WOULD SEEM to have been happy for the four brothers. Thomas Edward, the second of them, was born at Tremadoc in Caernarvonshire, Wales, on 15th August 1888. His father belonged to the Anglo-Irish Protestant landed gentry, his mother was a native of the north of Scotland.*

Ned was an active child full of vitality and vigour. He learned the alphabet at three years old by listening

* There had been a drama behind the life of the Lawrence family. The name Lawrence had been adopted and was not the real one. Sarah Maden, a puritanical young girl, became the governess in the family of Thomas Robert Chapman, a married man. Although a puritan by nature, she must have also been passionate since one day she went off with the master of the house who had lost his heart to her and with whom she fell in love. This union lasted all their lives, with absolute fidelity, but Mr. Chapman was unable to obtain a divorce and legalise their union. All this took place in Victorian times when such sins were regarded with the utmost severity, though others were treated indulgently enough. The pair cannot have led an easy life. To make things worse the young woman, who was henceforward to be known as Mrs. Lawrence, grew more and more puritanical instead of less and less so, on account of the irregular and, according to her religious beliefs, criminal condition into which she was bringing her sons into the world. Being very conscientious she felt condemned to a dreadful punishment for world without end. To try and propitiate fate she brought up her children on the most austere lines of rigid Protestant

to the lessons which were being given to his elder
brother. This showed that he was gifted with a good
memory and with the power of concentrating his attention. When he reached the age of rowdy games and of

morality. Of course the little boys knew nothing about their
parents' legal—or rather extra-legal—situation. Some critics who
have studied the work and character of T. E. have attributed his
sexual oddity, his chastity, quite abnormal in a man who held no
religious beliefs (though in my opinion he was full of a deeply
religious spirit and bible-fed from his childhood) his psycholo-
gical complexes and his suppressed desires, to a belief that at
about the age of ten he had discovered that his father and
mother were not married and that he himself bore an adopted
name. I do not reject the suggestion. Such a discovery may well
have left its mark on the child and consequently on the man.
It is not unlikely, given the character of our hero. His intelligence was able to rise above the facts, but his sensitive nature
made him vulnerable. The results of the trauma appeared later
on.

I got to know Mrs. Lawrence in 1946. The man who had been
her husband by love and spirit though not in the eyes of the law,
had died many years before and so had three of her sons, two of
them killed in the war of 1914, and the third, her Ned, in a
motor-cycle accident. I should not have been surprised if I had
learned that she secretly believed that she was to blame for these
catastrophes.

When I went to see her she was living modestly, indeed
humbly, with her eldest son Bob. At this first interview she
kindled such sympathy (no doubt because of her love for Ned)
and such respect (which she was herself sufficient to inspire) that
I never came to England afterwards without paying her a visit.
At the end she lived in a boarding house at Boars Hill near
Oxford. She had broken a leg and as often happens with old
people the bones would not join. This must have given her a
great deal of pain, but in the Lawrence fashion she appeared
not to notice it.

reading, no tree was too high for him to climb and no book too difficult for him to read. These two sides of Ned's character became more and more pronounced. He was capable, and forced himself to become capable,

---

The boarding house of two storeys had a narrow staircase such as you often find in old houses in England. Mrs. Lawrence's room was upstairs on the first floor. She explained that it was very convenient for when she needed Bob, who slept in the room directly underneath hers, she had only to knock on the floor with her stick. Bob ran up at once if he was there. Such was what Mrs. Lawrence understood by the word 'convenient'. Her broken leg, grown stiff, kept her almost immobile. The last time that I went to see her was in the middle of winter. One fire lit in the living room, in the only fireplace (very convenient also no doubt) took the chill off that room. It was really cold in Mrs. Lawrence's bedroom and the cheek on which I placed my farewell kiss was cold too.

During lunch which was frugal but served with such perfect cleanliness that it delighted me, there was a little incident which I thought revealing. Bob had written to London to invite me to Sunday luncheon, for on that day, he said, they had a particularly good meal. When I arrived about mid-day the sun was shining feebly. It was the anaemic sun of an English January. Nevertheless, Mrs. Lawrence was standing waiting for me at the entrance of the house supported by Bob on one side and her stick on the other. The country—so thickly inhabited that we should not call it country at all in Argentina—stretched all about us. Mrs. Lawrence was facing what one might have called a patch of garden. In it she had planted a few plants which, knowing her love for green things, I had sent her. She was looking at the corner in which bulbs and seeds were hiding under the earth from the cold.

Soon after my arrival the bell rang for lunch. We sat at a little table surrounded by other little tables at which the other lodgers at the boarding house took their places. As the second course they served, of all things, sago pudding of which I am

of intellectual achievements as well as physical ones. He
seems to have practised bodily endurance instinctively
and it appears always to have been the forced accom-
paniment, or the necessary complement, of the moral

very fond. I ate my helping and concealed my greed, but even
in front of the austere figure of Mrs. Lawrence could not prevent
myself from praising the dish and complaining of the difficulty
of tasting it except in England. Mrs. Lawrence asked me to
have some more. Very imprudently I replied: "Don't tempt
me," which in my own home would have been understood as,
"Yes, please." But she took my words literally and took them
as final. There was no way of inducing her to tempt me again.
It was not the slightest good repeating my praises and confessing
that I had a weakness for the pleasures of the table. It was
impossible to move her. She had some raw sago brought from
the kitchen so that I should see what it looked like and she gave
me the recipe for the pudding. But one refusal was enough.

Mrs. Lawrence talked to me about all her sons and in particular about Ned, with passion, but with a control which hid
her intense emotions. At such an age he already climbed the
tallest trees; at another he read books which would have little
appeal to a child of his age. Such things were told without
changing her voice or her expression, perfectly calmly as though
she were making a statistical report. In spite of her years which
were a heavy burden, her memories were fresh and her courage
unimpaired. She scarcely needed to turn to Bob to supply a
date, or an added detail, or find her a photograph or book
which she wanted to show me. Her inexhaustible memories kept
pace with my insatiable desire to hear more when the subject
was Ned.

I never heard her complain of anything or of any persons. It
seemed no effort for her to refrain from speaking ill of her
neighbour. Yet many things must have shocked her, for the
puritan in her was keenly alert. It was just the same with her
eldest son who shared, I think, her point of view. He knew that
I had translated *The Mint*. (And God knows that wasn't

laws which he willingly accepted. He did not develop
the weapon of his physical strength in order to break
the laws of a world which was not his; for him the will
of the stronger was never the better. One of his play-
mates describes how the Lawrence children amused

exactly a picnic owing to the difficulties of translation.) The
text is full of obscenities as the book gives a picture of barrack
room talk. There is an enormous obscene vocabulary in Spanish
and there was plenty to choose from. But I had to choose with
expert knowledge in order to be understood both in Spain and
throughout Latin America. Robert Lawrence had asked me in
a letter to make no allusion to *The Mint* in front of his mother.
"Neither she nor I have read it," and he underlined the words.

I know by hearsay that Mr. Lawrence was a very remarkable
man. But I suspect that without the Mrs. Lawrence I knew at
Boar's Hill there would have been no Lawrence of Arabia.
There was a vitality and an integrity in that woman which
were astonishing. And a strength greater than oak. She must
have lived in an inner hell during her youth. It must have been
like a foretaste on earth of what according to her moral and
religious code, was awaiting her in the next world. When I
talked to her at Boar's Hill these storms were over. Living almost
in poverty—I repeat poverty—with no wealth but her memories,
she had found peace, won by paying the price. It should be said
in passing that her contempt for money and other material
gratifications which the fame of her son could easily have pro-
cured her, was absolute. This attitude seems moreover to be
shared by all the members of this strange family. The fact of
having known Mrs. Lawrence and having received tokens of her
sympathy was a great honour for me. I owe it to the youngest
of the Lawrence family, A. W., the best beloved of T. E.'s
brothers. The resemblance between the two men is startling,
though they have reacted to life in different ways and their
experiences were very different. But in any case I do not believe
that any brother has understood his brother better than A. W.
has understood T. E.

themselves with others by playing a war game in an old orchard. There were two camps. The one led by Ned always won because he invented a species of hand grenade made of clay and flour which had devastating effects upon the other side. But he abandoned its use when he realised that it did not give them a sporting chance. Ned could not enjoy a victory unless it was founded on fair play. Organised games never interested him—which was strange in an English boy who wanted to make his body tough and fit enough to bear every fatigue and privation. If Ned did not, like Pascal, discover the elements of Euclidean Geometry for himself without a textbook, he read Macaulay's *Introduction to the History of England* with passionate interest when he was only eight years old, which is something quite unusual. His mother recalled that as a schoolboy his favourite books were a history of Egypt, Layard's book on the excavations at Nineveh and *Helps to the Study of the Bible*.

One day at school during the break he attacked a big boy who was maltreating a small one. In the fight which followed his leg was broken just above the ankle. It was eleven o'clock in the morning. Ned hopped back to the classroom holding on to the walls and sat through the mathematics lesson. At one o'clock he told his brothers that he could not walk and they pushed him home sitting astride his bicycle. The anecdote does not rank with that of the Spartan boy who let the fox gnaw his liver; nevertheless a broken bone is no joke.

This schoolboy fight, the reason for it and the way in which its results were borne in silence, are typical of Lawrence's behaviour in after life. As the years went by, his acts of physical endurance became heroic, frenzied, almost insane. The broken leg checked Ned's growth: he remained short, but extraordinarily strongly built.

Another of Ned's characteristics was that he liked to tell his brothers every evening an endless story about a besieged castle. He made it up as he went along. This reminds one of how the Brontë children spent their evenings in their little Yorkshire vicarage.

This endless daydream must have been handed on by little Ned to Colonel Lawrence and have obsessed him until it was translated into reality. Sometimes the recurrent rhythm of a dream may last till death, like a pulse beating in our blood. If it were possible to count the beats, to note how they go faster, to note all the details as the graph is traced on a chart of a man lying sick with fever, one might be able to foretell the final results of such a dream.

Lawrence was aware of the workings of those dreams which familiarise us with an event, prepare the ground for it and condition us to accomplish it, even though reason takes such overwhelmingly presumptuous forecasts as mere madness. In *Seven Pillars** he stresses this:

* From the introductory chapter suppressed in the original edition but included in the latest editions of *Seven Pillars*.

"All men dream: but not equally. Those who dream by night in the dusty recesses of their minds wake in the day to find that it is vanity; but the dreamers of the day are dangerous men, for they act their dream with open eyes, to make it possible."

To act his dream. That is what Ned had already begun to do when he sat with a broken leg through the mathematics lesson, when he gave up using clay hand grenades because they were not "fair play", when he read the history of England or the account of the excavations at Nineveh. Colonel Lawrence was to be indebted for many things to Ned.

Perhaps men owe their fame to the strength of the wave which carries them on its crest; but they are never great in themselves except so far as they have dreamed of being so in childhood, however circumstances may have favoured or frustrated such ambitions in later life. They cannot achieve success without a combination of favourable external elements but neither can they carry it to full fruition without the early dream. (The essence of complete realisation—or full fruition—has little to do with worldly success or worldly failure which are both due to external causes.) In Lawrence's case neither the dream nor the wave which was to carry him on its crest was lacking. Yet when the hour struck the exacting demands of his dream were to prevent his taking full advantage of the vast wave which would have carried him far upon its crest. For the wave was unworthy of the dream. It was always to be so.

In a letter to Kennington Lawrence wrote: "One of the sorest things in life is to come to realise that one is just not good enough. Better perhaps than some, than many, almost—but I do not care for relatives matching myself against my kind. *There is an ideal standard somewhere and only that matters: and I cannot find it.** Hence this aimlessness."

A man who feels that can only despise success and ends by feeling failure is a blessing. For the thing to which he aspires does not depend on external circumstance: he acts solely to achieve self-realisation. Thus no success could have satisfied T. E., for he was made of a different clay from a great artist or a great soldier. He was of the same stuff as the saints, and like them he had to find perfection within himself, and not like a great artist in the work he had conceived and executed. He had to feel that all his acts testified to the ideal standard at every moment. If they did not he had this feeling of emptiness and aimlessness.

* My italics.

THE YEARS OF TRAINING

IT HAD NEVER been enough for Ned to be fearless. He had also to be blameless. It is not easy to ride on the crest of the wave if you insist on both as essential. No one is born "fearless and blameless", "*sans peur et sans reproche*", in the way one is born of a fair or a dark complexion. Such qualities develop, or atrophy, like the muscles of the body. Exercise provides what the best natural disposition cannot achieve without it.

Ned knew that one could learn to conquer fear. When his baby brother, frightened by the statues in the Ashmolean Museum in Oxford, clung to him asking: "Are they alive?", he did not mock at the child's terror. After they had got home, he carved a grotesque face on a stone in the garden and gave the child a little hammer so that he could hit it too. And so the little boy learned not to be afraid of statues.

No one understood better than Lawrence how human it is to be afraid; no one was more understanding of the fears of other people. In a letter written in 1929 to Ernest Thurtle, M.P., he called for the abolition of the death penalty for cowardice on the field of battle. He who had born physical torture with an almost inhuman courage, wrote:

"I have run too far and too fast (but never fast enough to please myself at the time) under fire, to throw a stone at the fearfullest creature. . . ."

Lawrence was blameless because he was the first to blame himself. It is difficult to find any failing of which he had not accused himself. But he was not as innocent as the ordinary run of men, being more alert and quick and endowed with a more sensitive conscience.

Ned grew up in happy comradeship with his four brothers with no feminine influence but that of Mrs. Lawrence. Some people have wondered whether this helped to produce the suspicious and defensive attitude with which he regarded women—when thinking of them as members of the opposite sex and not simply as people. The hypothesis does not seem to me to have much basis since Lawrence's inhibition—if inhibition is the word for it—is not found in other families composed entirely of boys or of girls. Lawrence's distrust of women seems to me to be due to an inner attitude of mind which it is very hard to explain and not to external circumstances which might produce very different results in different individuals.

Ned attended Oxford High School from September 1896 until July 1907. From his early years he liked discovering and deciphering inscriptions on mediaeval tombs and he visited all the churches near Oxford and finally those all over England which were famous for their monumental brasses. He was just as keenly interested in ancient pottery, in cathedrals and in the ruins of ancient castles and he visited those in France on his bicycle during the holidays of 1906, 1907 and 1908. Then in the summer of 1909 he went to Syria where he spent three months after having already learned a smattering of Arabic. On this first journey to the East he was able to carry out his youthful plan of visiting and examining the castles built by the crusaders.

At Oxford Lawrence was well known for what his friend Chaundy called "his archaeological rummagings". He intended, indeed, to become an archaeologist.

Another of his friends tells us that what struck him most about Lawrence when he entered Jesus College, Oxford, was the brilliance of his blue eyes, his grin, and his charming voice. His small stature and his slenderness did not give much impression of physical strength. But he had not stopped cultivating it.

There is a story that about this period, he went one afternoon into a friend's rooms at Oxford and began firing a revolver out of the window into the street— luckily it was loaded with blank cartridges. This strange way of announcing his arrival revealed that he was in a state of violent over-excitement. In the conversation which followed, Lawrence said that he had just spent forty-five hours working continuously without taking food, in order to test his powers of endurance. Experiments of that sort, which he often made, might have been taken at that time for a student's boasting. But it must be said that without such training Lawrence would never have been able to impress the Arabs by showing that he had greater powers of physical endurance than they had. This soldier to be would not ask from others anything which he could not do himself. Moreover, perfect physical fitness was necessary for a young archaeologist who lacked money and wanted to do good work in Syria.

The study of the middle ages, of the crusades and of their influence in the western world, particularly in England, keenly interested him. He was mad about Gothic architecture and the construction of fortified castles. In 1911 he was delighted to accept an invitation to join the expedition which the British Museum was sending to Carchemish (Jerablus). He worked at those digs under Hogarth's orders; travelled across the north of Mesopotamia on foot, dug in Egypt and worked under Newcome's orders for the Palestine Exploration Fund, all between 1911 and 1914.

When war broke out he was twenty-six years old. The *Encyclopaedia Britannica* states that he was rejected for the army when he tried to enlist because he was below the standard in height, an amusing detail. He was then finishing his report for the Palestine Exploration Fund which Lord Kitchener wanted completed "pretty damn quick", according to Lawrence.

The author of *Seven Pillars* wanted a war job at all

costs, but they could find nothing better for him at the beginning than one in the map section of the War Office. Then Lord Kitchener sent him to Egypt to Military Intelligence. It was Lawrence who was responsible for the first number of *The Arab Bulletin* designed to keep the Foreign Office informed about what was going on in Arabia.

The moment when Lawrence's dream was to seem within his grasp was approaching. The idea of a British Empire made up of a voluntary association of self-governing states of all sorts of races, did not seem impossible to him. He had a special love for Arabia and wanted to see a renaissance of its culture and not to turn it into one more British possession. At last the opportunity came for him to attempt it while serving his own country at the same time.

THE ARAB REVOLT

"SOME ENGLISHMEN, OF whom Kitchener was chief, believed that a rebellion of Arabs against Turks would enable England, while fighting Germany, simultaneously to defeat her ally Turkey. Their knowledge of the nature and power and country of the Arabic-speaking peoples made them think that the issue of such a rebellion would be happy: and indicated its character and method. So they allowed it to begin, having obtained for it formal assurances of help from the British Government. Yet none the less the rebellion of the Sherif of Mecca came to most as a surprise, and found the Allies unready. It aroused mixed feelings and made strong friends and strong enemies, amid whose clashing jealousies, its affairs began to miscarry."

In these words Lawrence defines the origin of the Revolt of which he was himself to "indicate the character and method". He was its inspiration and its leader from 1916 to 1918. During these years of guerrilla fighting which he led with a skill and courage which brought victory, he won the friendship and the trust of the Arabs who fought with him and the esteem and admiration of his British commanders. His secret ambition was to convert both sides to his ideas. His public bitterness was because he had not fully succeeded in his hopes and because he fought in vain to make his country keep the promises which he had made the Arabs in its name. Having a double interest in the success of the campaign, he spared no effort to bring it to a successful issue. He lived among the Arabs, dressed as one of them and shared their privations and their dangers so long as the war lasted.

But all this would have been no more than a vague nimbus of glory attaching to the name of the young soldier if it were not for *Seven Pillars of Wisdom*. The enigma, the limelit figure which Lawrence had become, directly the war was over, and which had excited the ephemeral curiosity of press and public, would have soon been forgotten. No merits, no mysteries can hold the attention of those fickle monsters for very long. Lawrence's immense reputation might perhaps have lasted while he lived if he had not discovered in Bernard Shaw's words that: "Lawrence's genius included literary genius." After having lived the Revolt in the desert, he wrote it. And as Shaw also said, after Lawrence had lent him the manuscript, "the result was a masterpiece". By an ironic reversal of things, this masterpiece did not seem planned to please the press, or to be appreciated by a public which has not time to read 660 pages each one of which provides matter for thought.

Lawrence wrote once to his mother, when he was twenty-two, about great books:

"If you can get the right book at the right time you taste joys...which pass one out above and beyond one's miserable self, as it were through a huge air, following the light of another man's thought. And you can never be quite the old self again. You have forgotten a little bit: or rather pushed it out with a little of the inspiration of what is immortal in someone who has gone before you."

What is immortal in Lawrence—so far as humanity can perceive and appreciate immortality—is contained in *Seven Pillars of Wisdom* which holds the place in our lives which so many other great books held in his.

"It is almost terrible to think that your ideas, yourself in your books, may be giving life to generations of readers after you are forgotten."

It is indeed rather terrible. And that is the reason why the subject of a book, what the author has put into it, his attitude and what he is in himself, are not matters of no importance as some people pretend. *Seven Pillars* is a proof of it. Lawrence did not win the nickname of Prince Dynamite, which the Arabs gave him, without some sort of violent self-destruction. The man who dynamited trains packed with quivering human flesh—Turkish though it was—this dynamiter with a sensitive conscience shattered himself into fragments because of his need to suffer what he had inflicted upon others. The fragments of his inner self rain down upon the reader in some of the most extraordinary passages of his story. By comparison other pages are almost commonplace. He seems always to be waiting to find the last piece with which he can complete his real character and which will prove the key to the citadel. We don't need this last undiscovered bit to judge from the remainder that it was precious. But distress at leaving the puzzle for ever incomplete underlies the book. He infects us with it.

SEVEN PILLARS

A T FIRST *Seven Pillars of Wisdom* is a disconcerting title when one reflects that the book is the history of the desperate and finally triumphant struggle of the Arabs, supported by a few Englishmen and by Britain against the Turks—and of war with all its horrors. What connection can that struggle have with wisdom?

The title was inspired by the *Book of Proverbs* in the Bible where it is written: "Wisdom hath builded her house; she hath hewn out her seven pillars." Lawrence had chosen it, as a young man, as the title for a book on seven cities. He thought the book bad and it never appeared. The author made use of the title for his new book in memory of the earlier one.

Looking closer into the matter, one sees that the title is better suited to the second book which deals not with seven cities to be found on the map but with seven pillars of that moral world which Lawrence was aware of on the eve of battle when he was "shamed into pettiness by the innumerable silences of stars".

To the title there is added ironically a sub-title: *A Triumph*. A triumph when after the entry into Damascus he had that feeling of solitude and of absurdity? A triumph, that victory of which he said "only for me was the event sorrowful". A triumph, that "longing to be like these quiet ones", the dead lying under an indifferent sky?

The overt subject of the book is certainly the passion of war—that horrible game in which the will of the stronger is always right, in which the end justifies the means; that barbarous game which seems to perfect itself by growing more vile and by throwing away every shred of honour: war, the masterpiece of male creative genius.

The Arab Revolt in the desert was a magnificent subject for the man who had been its centre; and the young unknown archaeologist had been given a costly setting in a sumptuous frame.

But the essential subject, the underlying *leit-motiv* of *Seven Pillars,* is not the military campaign which was fought with such heroism and such brilliance.

"Please take it as a personal narrative pieced out of memory," says the author. From memory indeed since in December 1919 he lost his manuscript changing trains at Reading. But that is not all. "In these pages the history is not of the Arab movement, but of my part in it," he declares. That is the real subject. Lawrence, who was so unlike Montaigne, might like him have written at the head of his work: "Thus gentle reader, myself am the ground-worke of my booke." For what is staggering in the book is not the victorious expedition against Akaba, which brought the war in the

Hedjaz to an end, nor the 79 bridges that were dynamited, nor the railway line cut, nor the entry into
Damascus; it is him, himself, "always in the stretch or
sag of nerves", in a whirlpool of blood and sand. He
tells us in a note which precedes the synopsis that forty
other Englishmen might have written the same story.
Even admitting that these forty lived through the same
events as Lawrence with an equal fiery intensity (which
is extremely unlikely) it would have been necessary for
them to have been endowed with literary genius.
Heaven does not show itself so prodigal. The notes of
the scale belong to all alike, but only a few men can
compose music.

"There were many other leaders and lonely fighters
to whom this self-regardant picture is not fair," he
repeats. But what interests the reader in the story is the
author himself. Edward Garnett, who was one of the
first to read the first printing of *Seven Pillars,* blamed
Lawrence for not having given freer expression to his
intimate feelings.

"With whom are you comparing me?" Lawrence
asked him.

"With W. H. Hudson. In his books Hudson does not
hide his feelings," replied Garnett. To which Lawrence
answered: "Yes! But Hudson is above us all."

And indeed although *Seven Pillars* was actually written at white heat with passion, as its author says, one
is aware of constant restraint, of a fear of letting himself

go. It is a book written with the brakes on, like a car descending a mountain slope. One can feel the brake all the time even when the surface is level and there are no hairpin bends. This gets on the reader's nerves. An atmosphere of tension and constraint is created even although the machine is well oiled and there are no grinding noises.

Lawrence said that the essential things in the book are the personal revelations and that the personal chapter (Myself) is the key to it, but that it is in cipher. But why? He explains that it is "partly a constitutional inability to think plainly"—that is freely and without disguise—"and partly it's funk—or at least a feeling that on no account is it possible to think of giving myself quite away".

THE "HATEFUL I"

THE DISLIKE OF using the pronoun "I" in literature has always seemed to me a childish prejudice. In literature as in life the use of "I" may be hateful—but only when it happens to be so. The mere use of the first person singular is not hateful in itself. Egoism is no less hateful if it is represented by an indefinite "one" or a plural "we". Such use is merely playing with words, and I cannot see any sign of commendable modesty in these verbal pirouettes which are often employed by the most conceited authors. The poet says "I" in every verse. The novelist uses "I" out of his characters' mouths. The philosopher uses it under the cloak of his theories. The critic behind each of his objective judgments. And nothing would be of interest if it were otherwise. No work of art can be created except from a more or less sublimated or transposed "I". Otherwise we should have machines capable of writing masterpieces just as we have calculating machines. The idea of a machine able to write a masterpiece would not have displeased the Lawrence who said: "The fear of showing my feelings is my real self."

Whatever opinion he may have held about the "hateful I" he started hunting down the "I"s in *Seven Pillars* and replacing them with "we"s and "one"s. The substitutions could deceive nobody. For example in such passages as: "We were subject at the moment to the physical shame of success, a reaction of victory, when it became clear that nothing was worth doing and that nothing worthy had been done." The "I" crossed out below the "we" seems written in indelible ink. (Actually he never used that sort of ink.)

It is a curious experiment to compare *The Revolt in the Desert* with *Seven Pillars,* of which it is an abridgement. *Seven Pillars* is a book of about 280,000 words and *The Revolt* 130,000. *The Revolt* was a dish prepared for what Lawrence called "general consumption", and he has cut out everything to do with himself and his own emotions: the "I"s disguised as "we"s, or plain, the preface, the death of Farraj, the scene in the hospital, the camel killed in the charge, the chapter written on his birthday, etc.

"I cut out all high emotion."

What is there left? A dry book which one chews over and over interminably like coconut ice without being able to get it down. In spite of the descriptions in this story of real life being full of colour and written by a master, they must be classed as painted frescoes, like the magnificent battle scenes in Eisenstein's film *Alexander Nevsky.* They have the same splendid emptiness and the same cold perfection.

For readers who are not particularly interested in military exploits and war histories *The Revolt in the Desert* is—one must admit it—a dull book. While *Seven Pillars* may become one of the books from which one wishes never to be parted.

A STRANGE SOLDIER

Yes: this tale of war is unique for those who hate its subject. If it is possible to do an ignoble thing nobly —as it is to do a noble one ignobly—then that is how Lawrence made war.

It is common ground to repeat that he took the greatest risks and worst hardships on himself, that he was careful of his men's blood and economised their lives and that he was quick to admire good qualities in the enemy.

Thus—and the passage deserves to be stressed—he wrote of the Germans who fought against him with the Turks:

". . . and here for the first time I grew proud of the enemy who had killed my brothers.* They were two thousand miles from home, without hope and without guides, in conditions mad enough to break the bravest nerves. Yet their sections held together, in firm rank, sheering through the wrack of Turk and Arab like armoured ships, high-faced and silent. When attacked they halted, took position, fired to order. There was no haste, no crying, no hesitation. They were glorious." (Chapter CXVII.)

* Two of his brothers had been killed in the war.

A little more and one feels that Lawrence would
have stopped fighting to cheer them on. And that was
what a part of him—the looker-on—was doing.

He is never tender to the Turks, the enemies of his
great friends the Arabs. Their cruelty sickened him.
Descriptions of atrocities and of massacres abound in
Seven Pillars but one of the most striking is that in
which he describes the entry of his men into Tafas, an
Arab village which had been occupied by Djemal
Pasha's lancers. It was as still as death.

"Some grey heaps seemed to hide in the long grass,
embracing the ground in the close way of corpses. We
looked away from these . . . but from one a little figure
tottered off as if to escape us. It was a child, three or
four years old, whose dirty smock was stained red over
one shoulder and side, with blood from a large half-
fibrous wound, perhaps a lance thrust, just where neck
and body joined. The child ran a few steps, then stood
and cried to us in a tone of astonishing strength (all else
being very silent): 'Don't hit me, Baba.' Abd-el-Aziz,
choking out something—this was his village, and she
might be of his family—flung himself off his camel, and
stumbled, kneeling in the grass beside the child. His
suddenness frightened her, for she threw up her arms
and tried to scream, but, instead, dropped in a little
heap, while the blood rushed out again over her clothes;
then, I think, she died. We rode past the other
bodies. . . ."

These bodies were the bodies of women nailed down with bayonets in obscene attitudes and of dead babies looking very soiled.

Tallal, the Arab chief, the fine horseman so strong and courteous, "gave one moan like a hurt animal", Lawrence tells us. Then putting spurs to his mount he dashed at the enemy in a mad gallop. The distance was considerable. Both sides had stopped firing.

"Both armies waited for him and he rocked on in the hushed evening till only a few lengths from the enemy. Then he sat up in the saddle and cried his war-cry, 'Tallal, Tallal,' twice in a tremendous shout. Instantly their rifles and machine guns crashed out," and Tallal and his mare were riddled with hundreds of bullets. That day, by order of this young English soldier, for the first time during the war, they took no prisoners.*

* In this incident two things in Lawrence's reactions seem to me to be revealing. After the death of the child and the sight of the mutilated women, Tallal sat motionless upon his mare shivering as though in a fever. Lawrence went towards him to speak to him, but Auda caught his bridle and held him back. The fact that at that moment Lawrence felt the need to go up to Tallal shows that he was no longer watching himself. Auda had to give him a lesson in discretion since a mixture of pity and fury had mastered him. It also seems to me very significant that the central figure in this episode should be an insignificant little being whose bloody wound attracts and rivets Lawrence's attention in the midst of action. Although he did not leap from his camel like Abd-el-Aziz, one feels all through his description that he is mentally touching the child like him. One can set this

Lawrence had good reasons for not feeling particularly tender to the Turks yet he avoided, when he could, large scale massacres. "I held no great brief for them, but it was better they be not killed, if only to spare us the pain of seeing it."

On the eve of capturing Akaba one night after battle, while his men quarrelled over the loot and boasted of their deeds, he went back to the battlefield to see if the

scene beside what he describes to Lionel Curtis in a letter written in 1923 : one day Lawrence, who loved cathedrals, was lying on the turf gazing at Wells Cathedral. Not far from him a little girl dressed in white was playing with a ball, without a care in the world. She was so small that Lawrence says she looked "no more than a tumbling daisy at the tower-foot". He told himself that she was an animal, and in his morbid hatred of animal life he began to ask himself which he would sacrifice if he were forced to make a choice : the child or the cathedral? And he ends by admitting to himself that he would destroy the building to preserve that frail life. His choice seemed to him irrational, as irrational as the impulse which led him to risk his life and that of the friend with him in order to save a bird which dashed out its life against his sidecar. Instinctively he felt that all life was sacred and yet declared that had the world been his he would have left out animal life. He will not show his feelings, he forbids himself the slightest sign of emotion, but when he is caught unawares he betrays it in spite of himself. For example, when Kennington's little boy, aged two, walked barefoot on the gravel path his father was surprised to hear Lawrence cry out : "He'll hurt his feet! He'll hurt his feet!" Lawrence had not had time to protect himself; he had, one might say, slipped up on pity and lost his poise. So one can see that the despairing cry : "Don't hit me!" of the Arab child at Tafas must have pierced him like a sword.

dead had any clothes which could be of use for the wounded. But, following their usual custom, the Arabs had already stripped the Turkish corpses. Lawrence stopped beside them struck by the calm beauty of the dead. The moon shone down softening into ivory these white-skinned bodies, these young bodies. They were lying huddled in low heaps in such disturbing disorder that Lawrence felt that they could not find rest; rest which he felt he might give them. One by one he laid them out in order, straightening their limbs as though for sleep himself, "very wearied and longing to be of these quiet ones, not of the restless aching, noisy mob" that awaited him.

One might suspect another author of using Turkish corpses and Arab sufferings for literary effects. But if Lawrence wasn't one of the corpses it was not for want of risking his life.

He would never touch any of the money which *Seven Pillars of Wisdom* might have brought him. He felt that it was tainted. He would never accept rewards or honours for his part in the campaign. He would have felt ashamed of doing so. He was too clear-sighted to admire war "in which it is the duty of each of us to degrade himself", or to feel proud of himself while waging it. "I love the preparation and the journey and loathe the physical fighting", he wrote to a friend.

He detested the butchery of battle. But he forced

himself to live amidst it for two years for three reasons. Two of them became contradictory and tormented Lawrence excruciatingly. Between them they formed the hair-shirt which kept him unsullied, uncontaminated, and uncorrupted by the temptations of power and of honours.

SCRUPLES

Britain wanted the Arab rebellion against the Turks for victory on the Eastern front; Lawrence went to Arabia to work for this cause which was that of his country. But Ned went with him and Ned had dreamed "at the City School in Oxford of hustling into form, while I lived, the new Asia which time was inexorably bringing upon us". Ned was there fighting for another cause. And perhaps because his adolescent longings had been cloudy, the ideal country for which he wanted to fight was "one for which the human spirit had never found a name". In any case it was not called Great Britain nor were its frontiers those of the British Empire.

In the preface to *Seven Pillars*, suppressed in the published edition on the advice of Bernard Shaw (strange advice as it is one of the best chapters of the book) Lawrence lets Ned have his say and he gives the second reason:

"I meant to make a new nation, to restore a lost influence, to give twenty millions of Semites the foundation on which to build an inspired dream-palace of their national thoughts. So high an aim called out the inherent nobility of their minds, and made them play a generous part in events: but when we won, it was charged against me that the British petrol royalties in Mesopotamia were become dubious, and French Colonial policy ruined in the Levant. *I am afraid that I hope so.* We pay for these things too much in honour and in innocent lives."

Ned rebelled because he saw men of another generation—idealogically speaking—taking possession of the fruits of his victory and fitting them in to the old world which he had dreamed of transforming. It was for that transformation that he had shed his blood, suffered and fought.

"Youth could win, but had not learned to keep," he said. "We stammered that we had worked for a new Heaven and a new earth and they thanked us kindly and they made their peace,"—in the image and the shape of the old things youth hated the most.

Ned had not fought for such a peace. When he spoke of the young Englishmen who had fought beside him and of whom he was proud to be a compatriot, he was indignant that they were being sacrificed "not to win the war but that the corn and rice and oil of Mesopotamia might be ours".

It was essential to defeat the enemy. That was done, says Lawrence. But winning the war did not mean for him corn, rice and oil. He boasts as his chief glory that in "my thirty fights I did not have any of our own blood shed. All our subject provinces to me were not worth one dead Englishman."

What did he aim at, then? What was he working for, disguised as an Arab among Arabs and as an Englishman among Englishmen?

"If I have restored to the East some self-respect," he says, "a goal, ideals: if I have made the standard of rule of white over red more exigent, I have fitted these people in a degree for the new commonwealth in which the dominant races will forget their brute achievements, and white and red and yellow and brown and black will stand up together without side-glances in the services of the world."*

The statement is clear. He had proved during his years in Arabia that if a few men carried on the same work elsewhere, an understanding of that kind would become a possibility. But he reckoned too much on other Lawrences appearing.

In a document of November 1919 which has only recently come to hand and which A. W. Lawrence has made available to me, T. E. Lawrence enumerated his motives during the Arab Revolt as personal, patriotic, intellectual, and ambitious. "I liked a particular Arab and thought freedom for the race would be an acceptable present." He wanted to help win the war and Arab help reduced Allenby's losses by thousands.

* Is not that, today, the vision which inspires, and the only hope which sustains the United Nations?

Because he "was a half-poet" he didn't value material things much and the ideal, such as the impulse that carried them into Damascus, seemed the only thing worth doing.

His ambition was to widen Lionel Curtis's conception of the British Empire as a Commonwealth of free peoples to include an Arab Dominion in the Empire. "There is no other road for Egypt and India in the end."

But when they had captured Damascus the personal motive no longer existed since the Arab (S. A. no doubt) was dead. The patriotic aim was achieved for Turkey was broken and the war was won. The romantic desire to experience being the mainspring of a national movement had been surfeited by success. The political ambition to create Free Arab partners in the Commonwealth was not strong enough by itself to make him stay in the East, though it was the reason for his fight for Feisal in Paris and afterwards.

As the campaign proceeded his deep-rooted wish that a free united Arab people should be able to bring about a rebirth of their civilisation, as a necessary ingredient among others, grew steadily stronger. That was the freedom which he had promised the Arabs in the name of Great Britain. The Arabs would not have fought in order to pass from Turkish hands into those of the British and the French. Lawrence knew it. He knew also that the promises of his Government were undependable and he relied on the prestige of an Arab victory to enable him to insist upon their fulfilment.

Bit by bit things grew more tangled. Lawrence was torn between loyalty to his commanders and his country, and keeping faith with the Arab leaders and with the Arabs who had gone to their deaths because of their trust in his word and in his character. He was probably unable to talk with complete freedom of this inner conflict with either party. Stuck on the horns of this dilemma, Lawrence was already disgusted by glory founded on fraud, before his victorious entry into Damascus. He was thirty. On his birthday, the 15th August (and also that of Napoleon—a coincidence which pleased him as a child) this strange man of action wrote in a notebook in which he only made notes about his state of mind:

"It came to me queerly how, four years ago, I had meant to be a general and knighted, when thirty. Such temporal dignities (if I survived the next four weeks) were now in my grasp—only that my sense of the falsity of the Arab position had cured me of crude ambition."

Then a little later he adds:

"Here were the Arabs believing me, Allenby and Clayton (his commanders) trusting me, my bodyguard dying for me: and I began to wonder if all established reputations were founded, like mine, on fraud."

The inner humiliation resulting from that searching

examination of his conscience was an antiseptic which cured Lawrence of the fever resulting from an eager appetite for "temporal dignities". Though little inclined to give way to the temptations in Dante's first circles: lust, gluttony, anger and sloth (the sins of the flesh) Lawrence was on the other hand the destined prey of the sins of Lucifer, the great sins, on a grand scale, which spring from pride. The sins of the Angels. What he felt to be a failure was perhaps the saving of him. The bitterness of this failure saved him from falling to the level of a conqueror, or of a dictator, and becoming only able to sway the crowd but unable to sway those solitary, clear, exacting intelligences, those consciences which are, in all ages, the only foundation on which to rear the seven pillars of the temple which he sought so desperately.

"A leader who sees two sides cannot lead, cheaply, at any rate." That was one of the reasons for his apparent failure. It was impossible for him to do anything cheaply. And he saw both sides.

"Caenobite man may have as much influence as man social," he once said, "for example is eternal and the rings of its extending influence infinite."

It is as a monk that this man of action has kept his influence.

THE DEDICATION OF *SEVEN PILLARS*

THE THIRD REASON, Lawrence's personal motive underlying his campaign in Arabia (a development of the day-dream which began at Oxford High School), is mysterious. It is mentioned only twice by him: in the dedication to *Seven Pillars* and on its last page, but in exact terms, giving it as an all powerful spring of action.

Here is what he wrote himself about it to a friend: (It is to be noted that out of the 583 published letters this is the only one in which he mentions the subject.)

"S. A. (to whom *Seven Pillars* was dedicated) was a person now dead, regard for whom lay beneath my labour for the Arabic peoples. I don't propose to go further into the details thereupon."

We all of us know how the people who consort with us interpret our behaviour in different ways—often inaccurately. What can one say about the fatal results when they are trying to interpret a dedication like that of *Seven Pillars* which is hermetically sealed to exclude the light?

Naturally there has been much speculation about S. A. Some people suspect that he was a person entirely invented by Lawrence who always enjoyed a game of hide and seek, and wanted to lead the reader up the garden path. I don't think that that is at all likely.

In speaking of *Seven Pillars* to Garnett, Lawrence said: "Never was so shamelessly emotional a book."

It would be very strange if in an account made up partly of a truthful and objective history and partly of a clear subjective confession, Lawrence should have amused himself by introducing an uncalled for false touch of poetry, merely to tease, in a spirit of mystification.

The first edition of *Seven Pillars,* the only one which Lawrence would allow to be published during his lifetime, was a small limited edition of which only the author knew the exact number. It was a *de luxe* edition, part of which Lawrence gave to his friends. The rest went to subscribers at a very high price. And there had to be subscribers because the book was expensive and it was necessary to pay for its manufacture. But Lawrence, I repeat, would never touch a penny that the book brought in. To make the bibliophiles, whose attitude he disliked, despair, he refused to number this sumptuous edition. Thus *Seven Pillars* was to be read by a little group of friends for whom the author had a particularly high regard.

Why should he have wanted to put them on a false scent? What would a dedication addressed to an invented person have added or have subtracted from the value of the text? Why this red cloth, hiding nothing, being waved in front of the readers' eyes in order to make them charge it, as could be foreseen?

The other hypothesis is that S. A. was an Arab for whom Lawrence felt a deep friendship and who died before the end of the war.* I think this is much more reasonable. Naturally this hypothesis gives a handle to a thousand interpretations which are all the more

---

* Under the title *Oriental Assembly,* A. W. Lawrence published, after the death of his brother, the introductory chapter to *Seven Pillars,* suppressed on the advice of Bernard Shaw, as well as two long newspaper articles, photographs taken by T. E. Lawrence himself during the war, and some pages of a journal written in 1911 during an archaeological journey on the banks of the Euphrates. An entry in this journal dated 23 July states that a certain Shemali had brought a message from Dahoum with reference to the men working on the dig at Carchemish. Under the name Dahoum, A. W. Lawrence adds the following note : "Dahoum, who later became a great friend of T. E., was employed in the dig (at Carchemish) as a donkey-boy."

In a letter addressed on 24 June 1911 to Mrs. Lawrence he is mentioned in these terms : "The donkey-boy mentioned above (Dahoum) is an interesting character : he can read a few words of Arabic and altogether has more intelligence than the rank and file. He talks of going in to Aleppo to school with the money he has made out of us. I will try and keep an eye on him, to see what happens." In 1913 Lawrence took the foreman of the dig and Dahoum back with him to Oxford. The young man died during the war and appears to have had most of the characteristics of S. A. to whom Lawrence dedicated *Seven Pillars.* "An imaginary person of neutral sex", said the author in a note. That is all we know precisely of the origin of the mysterious S. A.

untrue because they are made by people incapable of living, or of imagining that anyone can live at Lawrence's pitch.

I am far from believing like Carlyle that to understand is to show oneself equal. One can understand a tragedy by Shakespeare or a fugue by Bach and be completely unable to write like Shakespeare or to compose like Bach. To understand is not to equal. It is, rather, a synthesis of intelligence and of love when faced with a person or a work. A synthesis which is sometimes so miraculous that it deceived Carlyle as to its nature. This synthesis is indispensable for those who wish to approach Lawrence's inner citadel imaginatively, which is all the more difficult for us to do because it seems as though it had been equally difficult for him.

On the last page of *Seven Pillars,* in speaking of the motives which led him to undertake the campaign in Arabia, he wrote: "The strongest motive throughout had been a personal one, not mentioned here, but present to me, I think, every hour of these two years. Active pains and joys might fling up, like towers, among my days: but, refluent as air, this hidden urge re-formed, to be the persisting element of life, till near the end. It was dead before we reached Damascus."

If Lawrence mentions such an important personal motive it is because he wishes the reader to know of it; he wants to perpetuate the memory, "at least so long as pen and book shall live . . ."* This seems to me to be undeniable. That he wished to conceal the identity of the person who was the secret mainspring of his action cannot be doubted. I would as soon think of opening a letter that was not addressed to me as try to uncover a secret of that kind.

In consequence I only touch on the dedication so far as Lawrence has allowed me to do so by having set it on the threshold of such an authoritative and serious book as *Seven Pillars*. For it is authoritative and serious as regards matters of conscience. I deal with the dedication only in so far as I find it necessary to explain how my point of view can be reconciled with the various theories, or how far it differs from them.

> "I loved you, so I drew these tides of men into my hands
>   and wrote my will across the sky in stars
> To earn you Freedom, the seven pillared worthy house,
>   that your eyes might be shining for me
>   When we came."

That is how the dedicatory poem begins. "The seven pillared house"; we must not forget that the seven pillars are those of the Temple of Wisdom.

"To earn you Freedom." What sort of freedom is meant? We know what Lawrence meant by national freedom, if it is that. But if it is applied to a person and if the word "freedom" when he is thinking of others

* Ronsard. Sonnets.

means what it means when he is thinking of himself, we must be on our guard. He declares that he has rejected free will, authority, action, the senses, intellectual life and honours because he had fathomed their futility. "They were all failures." There is left, he says, obedience. And he set out to look for this new form of liberty in the lowest ranks of the R.A.F. driven there perhaps by his daemonic pride. There he would find relief from any responsibility by undertaking a menial job which he could only get by changing his name and disguising himself again. But he is already afraid that obedience has provided only an illusion, the misleading mirage of what he is seeking. And that his perpetual disappointment with each thing that he tries and each change that he makes is due to something in himself. That the failure is only in him.

He is looking for freedom. And he wants to give it to others. Freedom which he thinks he will obtain by giving up everything else. He knows that it can only be won by such a propitiatory sacrifice—since appetites which have accepted the pleasures of the flesh, or of earthly possessions such as money, power and honours tie you down with their formidable lilliputian army with its cords and pegs. He has annihilated the greater part of his appetites. He fights and gains victory over them all. And yet his daemon is a prisoner suffering the torments of the damned because it is living in the deepest pits of hell. Owing to his daemonic pride he tries to find in freedom what is only the gift of love. Freedom itself evades him because he asks from it what it has not got to give; because he is seeking liberty in a category of things in which it is not to be found—because liberty is never free enough, or justice sufficiently just for those who have an unlimited need and unlimited demand, even if it is unavowed, for super-human love.

The saint does not need either liberty or justice for himself. He does not need justice from men because all he asks is to suffer for their sake; he does not need to be given freedom, his aim is to achieve freedom of another kind. He is not against liberty and justice but is above needing them for himself. Lawrence was all for liberty and justice. He wished to dispense them and to receive them. But as he looked closer, he felt that they were not sufficient for him and he blamed himself for having taken the wrong road, inasmuch as he sought satisfaction in what was by its nature incapable of providing him with it.

Lawrence once wrote to Edward Garnett that he had collected a shelf of the titanic works of literature: *The Brothers Karamazov, Thus Spake Zarathustra* and *Moby Dick* and that his ambition had been to add an English fourth to it.

"You will observe that modesty comes out more in the performance than in the aim," he added slyly.

The exact opposite is true of his moral life, of that

search for freedom for which he was ready to sacrifice everything. In spite of himself he lived on a higher plane than he aimed at. That was why the goal he had envisaged could never satisfy him when he had reached it.

To which kind of freedom, then, did he allude in the dedication? If it were addressed to an Arab it was certainly the material freedom which he dreamed of restoring to that people. If it were addressed to an imaginary being—to some phantom—to a vague divinity within or outside himself—it is certainly that spiritual liberty which I have been discussing. But the verses which follow, dealing with death, render the first hypothesis more probable than the second.

> "Death seemed my servant on the road, till we were near and saw you waiting :
> When you smiled, and in sorrowful envy he outran me and took you apart
> Into his quietness.
>
> Love, the way-weary, groped to your body, our brief wage ours for the moment
> Before earth's soft hand explored your shape, and the blind worms grew fat upon
> Your substance."

The line "Before earth's soft hand explored your shape" does not suit a spectre. The body "ours for the moment" which will be given to the blind worms doesn't seem to me to belong to a phantom. The last lines, however, have a poetical intensity which—though the approach is very different—makes one think of the poems of *Gitanjali* in which the Creator and his created creature seem inextricably entangled.

> "Men prayed me that I set our work, the inviolate house
>   as a memory of you.
> But for fit monument I shattered it, unfinished : and now
> The little things creep out to patch themselves hovels
>   in the marred shadow
>   Of your gift."

Those are the accents in which other poets address a divinity—whether He be vague or realised. They are the accents of Tagore—translated into English by himself, or into French by Gide. But God is strictly banished from Lawrence's vocabulary as He is from that of many of our contemporary writers in whom, in spite of that, we find an almost religious awareness of the problems of humanity and the mystery of the universe.

ASCETICISM

LAWRENCE WENT FURTHER. He rediscovered the efficacity and value of certain religious austerities which he put into practice. For example: sexual continence. Of course chastity did not have the same significance for Lawrence that it has for a monk and he did not practise it in the same spirit. In his eyes it ranked with his habit of only drinking water (he maintained that water could have more varied flavours than wine), of eating only the necessary minimum, and of being equally frugal of sleep—except when a need arose to sacrifice eating and sleeping for some cause—such as the campaign in Arabia when he was living in it, or later writing about it.

Women, in so far as they were females, he seems to have regarded with distrustful contempt. But in so far as they were human beings, and if he felt they merited it, with the same respect and affection which he gave his men friends. He did not wish to get involved with lust any more than with sloth and gluttony—or with wealth which leads to them. All such temptations were a good excuse for the exercise of his will, and of proving to himself that he was the master of his appetites. He carried this so far that at one time he forbade himself music, which he loved almost as much as his books. This was in 1923 when he had hidden himself in the tank corps at Bovington Camp. He wrote then to Lionel Curtis about his disgust for everything partaking of carnality and sexuality which the obscene talk in barracks presented to his imagination.

"I react against their example into an abstention even more rigorous than of old. Everything bodily is now hateful to me (and in my case hateful is the same as impossible)."

That last parenthesis is pure Lawrence: for him "hateful" is a synonym of "impossible". The conversations of his companions about women, their cries in dreams during the night, acted on Lawrence as an anti-aphrodisiac. That is a reaction that a woman is much better able to understand and share than a man, that is if she has retained a delicacy of feeling which has not been deadened by prostitution in any of its forms. For whoever uses another's prostitution, or accepts it as inevitable, by that very fact, is prostituting himself. I would say in passing, that prostitution is a tree with many branches and that their shadow falls on many things that seem remote from its trunk.

In any case Lawrence had kept an uncommon delicacy of feeling.

In the same letter to Curtis he explains that he has denied himself music though he is so starved for it "that even a soldier stumbling through a song on the piano makes my blood run smooth. (I refuse to hear it with my head.)"

That is another revealing parenthesis. Lawrence's will, that consuming will-power which forced him to do what he most hated, controlled his head, but not his blood. That is the reason why he hated everything which was allied to his blood and would not submit itself like his conscious intelligence to the orders of his will. Lawrence asks himself if this is not madness due to his having forced himself to stay at Bovington Camp which hurts him and of forcing himself to endure life in barracks willingly "till the burnt child no longer feels the fire".

"Do you think," he asked Curtis, "that there have been many lay monks of my persuasion? One used to think that such frames of mind would have perished with the age of religion: and yet, here they rise up, purely secular."

What a mystery that generation to which Lawrence belonged was! Men without religious faith, but who threw up explorers of the spirit, men ready to embark like Columbus on his first voyage, but without the hope of finding new trade routes or new continents, but ready to repeat such heroic exploits for their own sake, with no ulterior object. All that they had kept from their legacy of the ages was a "divine sense of direction";* they would not admit it was more than the

* Claudel. *Feuilles des Saints. Sainte Thérèse.*

instinct of the homing pigeon and ignored the message that the bird carried under its wing.

For every reason I think it matters little whether the words: "I loved you", in Lawrence's dedication were addressed to an abstract idea or to the human incarnation of one. In either case the fervour with which it had been written was the same: a fervour which can sustain and render us capable of enterprises which we could not have attempted or succeeded in, lacking it.*

* Compare : "Fear, the strongest motive in slothful man, broke down with us, since love for a cause, or for a person, was aroused. For such an object, penalties were discounted, and loyalty become open-eyed, not obedient. To it men dedicated their being, and in its possession they had no room for virtue or vice. Cheerfully they nourished it upon what they were; gave it their lives and greater than that the lives of their fellowship : it being many times harder to offer than to endure sacrifice."

Seven Pillars. Chap. LXXXIII

HOMOSEXUALITY

IN LITERATURE HOMOSEXUALITY is always the occasion for detailed grandiloquent justifications and scientific reflections, or of obscure unclean explanations mixed up with a sense of guilt, or of weakness which turns to bragging. You apologise and then preen yourself upon it.

In the first pages of *Seven Pillars*, which are among the most beautiful in the book, there is less than a page on the subject, about the sex life of the men taking part in the Revolt in the desert. I have never read, on a subject of that kind, anything so frank, so direct and so free from self-satisfied lewdness. The first time that I opened the big book and turned over the first chapters, my eyes were caught by this page and my surprise was extreme. What did such a tone imply?

"The men were young and sturdy; and hot flesh and blood unconsciously claimed a right in them and tormented their bellies with strange longings. Our privations and dangers fanned this virile heat, in a climate as racking as can be conceived. We had no shut places to be alone in, no thick clothes to hide our nature. Man in all things lived candidly with man.

"The Arab was by nature continent; and the use of

universal marriage had nearly abolished irregular courses in his tribes. The public women of the rare settlements we encountered in our months of wandering would have been nothing to our numbers, even had their raddled meat been palatable to a man of healthy parts. In horror of such sordid commerce our youths began indifferently to slake one another's few needs in their own clean bodies—a cold convenience that, by comparison, seemed sexless and even pure. Later, some began to justify this sterile process, and swore that friends quivering together in the yielding sand with intimate hot limbs in a supreme embrace, found there hidden in the darkness, a sensual co-efficient of the mental passion which was welding our souls and spirits in one flaming effort. Several thirsting to punish appetites they could not wholly prevent, took a savage pride in degrading the body, and offered themselves fiercely in any habit which promised physical pain or filth."

The tone of those lines pulled me up sharply. I knew nothing of the book, or of Lawrence's personality. The title of the book had seemed to me presumptuous and the number of pages unnecessary. I was out of patience with him before I began ... But the tone of that passage left me silent. As though, suddenly, a voice compelled me to listen without replying a word, so that I could listen better. I did not know then that Lawrence was among those "thirsting to punish appetites they could not wholly prevent".

But I knew already, since the tone of that passage could not have been faked, that the book was about something very different from a campaign in the desert, something different from sanguinary and picturesque incidents, quite different from looting and lust and camels and dynamite. Or rather that, amidst all those, there was something very different shining through. The warlike, clamorous, thrilling background was dust thrown in the reader's eyes; it was actually only the opportunity of stating that "Man could rise to any height. There was an animal level beneath which he could not fall."

Farraj and Daoud were two boys in the Arab Army.

"They were an instance of the Eastern boy and boy affection that the segregation of women made inevitable," Lawrence says. And he adds: "Such friendships often led to manly loves of a depth and force beyond our flesh-steeped conceit. When innocent they were hot and unashamed. If sexuality entered, they passed into a give and take, *unspiritual relation*,* like marriage."

That is what Colonel Lawrence's relations with the person to whom *Seven Pillars* is dedicated were not. Whether you call such a feeling love or friendship, it was not a coarse exchange of mutual services. No relationship other than a spiritual one could have inspired that dedication.

"... the inviolate house, as a memory of you ..."

* My italics.

The monument which lasted, and which is *Seven Pillars of Wisdom* much more than it is the Arab Revolt, and the need to immortalise the memory of S. A. whose initials are written at the beginning of the book, is built of love. Of that love which in man already is addressing something which transcends our human state since it seems to say: "What have I to do with anything which is not immortal!" Of that love which thinks only in terms of eternity. And if Lawrence shatters the monument in order that it should be fitting, it is because that monument can only be completed in a world where there is nothing any longer of which death can rob us.

NOTE. It has occurred to me as an afterthought that if there had been any obvious tendency to homosexuality it would have been seen by the R.A.F. and T. E. would have been discharged immediately. I have been informed that T. E.'s hut companions have borne witness to its absence.

THE FLESH

To rediscover the efficacity of the ascetic life outside the religious rules which exact its observance, to discover the virtues of a love "that outlasts the sun and the ever fixed stars", outside the promises of rewards or punishments in another world, or hope of paradise which makes up to us for suffering, or fear of hell which punishes us; to know here on earth the joys and the torments of souls which call themselves heavenly or infernal, such seems the destiny of a few men in this century. Perhaps they are condemned to die, like Christopher Columbus, without knowing on what continent they are stranded.

Lawrence was expiating in the earthly hell of his own conscience the sin of Dante's eighth circle—that in which Ulysses expiates his deceit and wiliness as well as courage. Lawrence was accusing himself of being, like Ulysses, a false counsellor and was in torment. Lawrence was voluntarily hiding anonymously in a barracks because that was his hair shirt. What are we to call this need, this central drama of his life, which is also the need and the drama of an agnostic *élite* which cannot, honestly, help being that?

Sadism, masochism, neuroses, suppressed desires,

complexes, all those things which psychoanalysis invents in order to debunk the scruples and ardent aspirations of mankind and their rebirth in secular disguises, are not sufficient to explain them. Or they only explain them completely to those who feel contempt for religious fanaticism, are blind to everything in religion except its fanaticism, and like an untrained cyclist tumble into the hole which they are trying to avoid—that is into scientific fanaticism.

It is obvious that Lawrence's attitude to women as revealed in what he said and wrote and how he behaved during his life, is a splendid field for analysis of this kind. It is also true that there were suppressed desires and complexes in him. But the results arrived at by psychoanalytical methods are paltry and are incapable of embracing the subject, of containing or coming to grips with it. Must one think, then, that some suppressed desires and complexes are necessary, like scions grafted upon the stock, so that the human tree may bear rare and delicious fruit?

In *Seven Pillars* we find an anecdote about Auda, the chief of an Arab tribe, which throws light on Lawrence's psychology in regard to the female sex. One day, bursting like a thunderclap into the tent of his friend and companion in arms, he discovered him in the loving company of his latest wife, who bolted like a rabbit out of the way of the unexpected visitor. Lawrence took advantage of this happy occasion to utter a joking reproof. He pretended to be astonished that the grand old man should be as crazy as the rest of his race in thinking of "our comic reproductive processes, not as an unhygienic pleasure, but as the main business of life". One can imagine how sick Auda must have felt at his dalliance being cut short! He replied that he wanted heirs. At these words Lawrence pretended deep surprise. Had Auda found life so good that he wanted to pass such a dubious present on to someone else? Lawrence's tone was playful, but he was expressing the fixed idea which we find in his letters. Auda cannot have looked much like Ophelia, but Lawrence was playing the scene in Hamlet: "Get thee to a nunnery: why wouldst thou be a breeder of sinners?"*

For Lawrence, like Hamlet, thought that women are dangerous: "for wise men know well enough what monsters you make of them."†

Lawrence could also see in women human beings as worthy of his asexual friendship as men.

"Women? I like some women," he wrote to Ernest Thurtle. "I don't like their sex: any more than I like the monstrous regiment of men. Some men. There is no difference I can feel between a woman and a man. They look different, granted: but if you work with them there doesn't seem any difference at all. I can't

* *Hamlet*. III. i.   † *Hamlet*. III. i.

understand all the fuss about sex. It's as obvious as red hair: and as little fundamental, I fancy."

Or he saw females, coveted by males, as the snares of that lust which made his comrades in the barracks, the men in Hut No. 12, cry out in their troubled sleep. That lubricity exacerbated his disgust and contempt for the flesh.

"I lie in my bed," he wrote to Lionel Curtis, "night after night with this cat-calling carnality seething up and down the hut, fed by fresh matter from twenty lecherous mouths . . . and my mind aches with the rawness of it."

He writes to the same friend that everything with flesh in its mixture, everything which is created, is the achievement of a moment when the lusty thought of Hut 12 has passed to action and conceived.

"You wouldn't exist, I wouldn't exist, without this carnality," he says gloomily.

Everything connected with the flesh came to seem base and odious to Lawrence. He declares that categorically at the end of one of the most important chapters of his book. In speaking of his comrades he wrote:

"Also they were interested in so much that my self-consciousness rejected. They talked of food and illness, games and pleasures with me, who felt that to recognise our possession of bodies was degradation enough, without enlarging upon their failings and attributes. I would feel shame for myself at seeing them wallow in the physical which could be only a glorification of man's cross. Indeed the truth was I did not like the 'myself' I could see and hear."*

The subject of all the soldiers' talk between waking and sleeping, was an animal appetite, which, if they weren't too particular, they could satisfy on the day of leave and which they satisfied in imagination during the rest of the week. For these soldiers woman was the fighting man's diversion in the most primitive meaning of the words. Living in this atmosphere, Lawrence grew more and more exacerbated by these unappetising forms of sexual indulgence. He saw lust at that time in every union between man and woman in which sex played a part. Before then, in the desert, he had asked a newly married Arab, Abd-el-Mayin, how "they could

* "It was this horror of the physical intimacies he never experienced with anyone—we have his word for it—which inspired his abstinent habits," explains his brother A. W. Lawrence. (*T. E. Lawrence by His Friends*). It is clear that T. E. Lawrence's chastity was rather a reflex than a heroic virtue. Reflexes are not chosen; they are not adopted with deliberation. In the chapter entitled "Myself" in *Seven Pillars* there is a very significant passage about Lawrence's physical reactions.

"To put my hand on a living thing was defilement and it made me tremble if they touched me or took too quick an interest in me. This was an atomic repulsion, like the intact course of a snowflake. The opposite would have been my choice if my head had not been tyrannous. I had a longing for the absolutism of women and animals and lamented myself most when I saw a soldier with a girl, or a man fondling a dog, because my wish was to be as superficial, as perfected; and my jailer held me back."

look with pleasure on children, embodied proofs of their consumed lust?"

Like all his feelings, his repugnance for the fruits of the flesh was extreme, but it is easy for me to understand it. Lust is a fleeting passion; it does not ask for eternity. It needs but a moment for the begetting of the immortal being which is the child. And from that moment lust has nothing further to do with it. Only men on the level of mere animals feel no horror in the idea of giving eternal life to a moment of fleeting lust. And Lawrence who saw nothing in the union of the sexes but an act of lust, was unable to admit that one should glorify the results. Who, in such a state of mind and with such a point of view would not have felt the same?

Lawrence went out of his way not to understand that between a man and a woman there can be something more than an animal physical attraction, something more than a fervent friendship and deep esteem, something more than a physical preference and an intellectual affinity. There can be love in the most complete form known to humanity: the Love between man and woman who by the laws of their nature are neither angels nor animals. In such love the communion of the flesh is a materialisation of the longing for eternity which each lover wants for the other. In such love the immortality of the flesh—in the shape of the child—is an element.

> Make thee another self for love of me
> That beauty still may live in thine or thee.*

This other self is not the result of consummated lust as Lawrence declared. It is the prolongation of him or her whom with our feeble human resources each has wished to deliver from death. It is the resurrection of the flesh on earth.

Shakespeare, who besides his poetic genius had a sensual genius which Lawrence lacked, understood this and expressed it in his sonnets.

> Against this coming end you should prepare
> And your sweet semblance to some other give.†

Lawrence thought Shakespeare "the greatest of poets and the most consummate master of vowels and consonants, but as a philosopher and moralist I've no abnormal respect for him".

What I think escaped Lawrence—for one can only read into an author what one might have written oneself had one been born with his gift of expression—was Shakespeare's vast and violent sensual genius which speaks through the mouths of Juliet and Othello. The rapture of the young creatures whose love carries them to the height of sacrifice, the tragedy of the Captain whose jealousy plunges him into the depths of madness,

---

* Shakespeare Sonnets. XI.
† Shakespeare Sonnets. XIII.

the ardour, the insane despair packed with the beauty and the tumult of the earth are born of that genius. And Shakespeare's grandeur with them. The sensual and spiritual grandeur of a poet who can unite in a single phrase "those things which groan at being put asunder"* and for whom a final resurrection includes that of the flesh.

* Claudel. *Feuilles des Saints. Ode Jubilaire....*

FAITH, LOVE AND WILL

IN LAWRENCE, SOUL and body did not "groan at being put asunder" but at being shamefully intermingled and interdependent.*

* I doubt if Lawrence could have thought of the resurrection of the flesh except with horror and it was for such reason that in him body and soul groaned at being united. In Chapter LXXXIII of *Seven Pillars* he wrote:

"The conception of antithetical mind and matter, which was basic in the Arab self-surrender, helped me not at all. I achieved surrender (so far as I did achieve it) by the very opposite road, through my notion that mental and physical were inseparably one: that our bodies, the universe, our thoughts and tactilities were conceived in and of the molecular sludge of matter, the universal element through which form drifted as clots and patterns of varying density. It seemed to me unthinkable that assemblages of atoms should cogitate except in atomic terms. My perverse sense of values constrained me to assume that abstract and concrete as badges, did not denote oppositions more serious than Liberal and Conservative. The practice of our revolt fortified the nihilist attitude in me. During it, we often saw men push themselves or be driven to a cruel extreme of endurance: yet never was there an intimation of physical break. Collapse rose always from a moral weakness eating into the body, which of itself, without traitors from within, had no power over the will. While we rode we were disbodied, unconscious of flesh or feeling, and when at an interval this excitement faded and we did see our bodies, it was with some hostility, with a contemptuous sense that they had reached their highest purpose, not as vehicles of the spirit, but when, dissolved, their elements served to manure a field."

Hateful and impossible were for him synonyms, and the physical had become hateful. His willing and powerful body, even if fainting and exhausted, unfortunately made of flesh and bone and not of steel like a Rolls-Royce engine, obeyed his impetuous and implacable will. It obeyed him as best it could, but sometimes it could only hobble after him. Only on one occasion did his body refuse at the very last, to obey his frenzied will. It gave in to torture and Lawrence wrote: "In Deraa that night the citadel of my integrity had been irrevocably lost."

To achieve that the Turks had flogged him to within an inch of his life: he had become a bleeding rag of flesh in their hands. They had taken him for a Circassian deserter and his white skin had aroused the Bey's lust; to which he had refused to submit in spite of threats. But the experience of having been broken until he wept with pain, and of having screamed for mercy was to pursue him as the most burning humiliation.

Lawrence demanded from his body what the saints seem to be able to attain: the capacity to suffer martyrdom. According to David Garnett, Lawrence's most abnormal characteristic was his desire and readiness to suffer. You must be anaesthetised by religious faith in order to endure martyrdom: but Lawrence sought it with no anaesthetic but his unmerciful will. But even a monstrously hypertrophied will like Lawrence's is not strong enough to replace religious faith. It is only faith that can move mountains. "Verily I say unto you if ye have faith like a grain of mustard seed."

If you haven't the grain the mountains stay in their places and martyrdom is impossible. The kind of anaesthesia produced by religious faith cannot be brought on by a stiffening of will power.

Even without faith you may become unable to feel such things as fatigue if your whole attention is riveted on something. Thus the gambler can stand for hours beside the green cloth without knowing that he is exhausted. A mother can pass nights without sleep watching over her sick child. In such cases the body seems forgotten. Such things are paid for later, but while they last they are miraculous. But the gambler's passion which is a vice, and the mother's passion for her child which is one form of love, are very far from religious faith which is not one form of love but love itself. Is it strange that religious faith works miracles when intensely strong human passion can show the first signs of a miracle not only in forgetting the body momentarily and enduring fatigue, but in its being blotted out altogether? Lawrence wished to perform miracles with nothing but his will. Did he not know that although the body may be broken in, it cannot be forgotten? The will can master the beast in us: only love can drive it out. Lawrence was denied that blessing.

He was right to feel instinctively how great the danger was for a man who had been called to accomplish great tasks, of having loves and ties in the flesh. Inevitably the day comes when Abraham is asked to sacrifice Isaac; Abraham will always be tested by being told to choose between his son and God. Those who refuse to have an Isaac avoid a temptation and a snare into which it is too easy to fall: for Isaac's life may be more precious than one's own salvation. That is how personal immortality in one's child exacts its price.

And the angel who catches Abraham's arm with the uplifted knife always leaves him time in which to suffer an agony worse than death. How very different are these sufferings and these joys of the flesh and the spirit from lust! As different as love which sets on fire all that it transposes and transforms.

MACHINES AND MUSIC

LAWRENCE WAS RIGHT in thinking that women cannot understand machinery. They are excluded from the machine cult and it is safe for a man to take refuge in the temples where it is worshipped without fear of being disturbed by the presence of women.

No transformations or transpositions are possible with machines. You are at peace with them. A crankshaft is a crankshaft, a boiler is a boiler, a nut a nut. Whereas with women one can be sure of nothing, not even that lust is lust and friendship, friendship. Not even that the body is attentive when the soul is wandering. Or that the soul is enthralled if the body is not. Everything in them is diffused—using the word as one does for light which will not throw sharp shadows—because everything in them carries its message. Their love is sensuality as often as their sensuality is love. At the moment when you think you see the outline of a feeling defined, it is already dissolving and changing into something else. The senses are so close to the soul that the flesh and the spirit, bewildered by their meeting, have no words in which to explain it. Music alone can speak of such encounters—but women don't compose it, perhaps because it is too like the substance of

their lives. Men dream of it and from that noble un-
satisfied dream is born their music which tells its story;
—that noble fluid thing which knows no barriers—their
music.

Lawrence was afraid of music (at the moments when
he denied himself it) rather as he feared women.
Because he knew that in music, as in woman, a nut is
not always a nut. That the notes of the octave may be
a garden where it is raining, a house in a distant town,
waiting, desire, a sudden glance, the flavour of a forgotten day in April, triumph, despair, prayer, our
childhood, those features, that love, everything that
time and space wipes out and which remains unchanged
in it. That they are seven witnesses which remind us
of our joys and sorrows, retold by them with faithful
sweetness. That it is vain to question them in turn in
order to learn their mystery;—for their mystery is that
they can only speak when they melt and vanish into
one another.

However, Lawrence did not deny himself music,
except at rare moments. It was not cut out of his life.
Music tamed him and if he was possessed by anything
besides his will, it was by music. The list of records pre-
served in his little cottage at Clouds Hill is very long
and chosen with a rare good taste. We can tell how he
loved music by a note in a letter which he wrote to Mrs.
Thomas Hardy on the death of her husband, who was
a dear friend of Lawrence's.

"This is Sunday and an hour ago I was on my bed listening to Beethoven's last quartet, when one of the fellows came in and said that T. H. is dead. We finished the quartet, *because all at once it felt like him . . .*" The Beethoven quartet had suddenly become Thomas Hardy and all that Lawrence felt for him. A nut was no longer only a nut. The world of music, fluid, moving, and without barriers had taken Lawrence's emotion into itself, and had closed round it as the water closes round a diver. And wrapped in it Lawrence was closer to Hardy than he could have been outside.

Machines at that moment would not have offered him a refuge as music did. And one wonders why he was willing to give himself up to such *excursions of the spirit* (that is what Beethoven was for him) in which his will did not play the chief part, as it did usually.

CONTRASTS

LAWRENCE ONLY ESCAPED from his totalitarian will power, which would otherwise have pulverised him, thanks to the contradictions in his nature. He inevitably lived in a world of contrasts and his capacity for seeing both sides of a question and of taking first one and then the other point of view acted like a safety valve. He thought that the best definition of himself, Edward Garnett's, was: "a critic in action."

One night Lawrence went to blow up a bridge and found it held by the enemy. He saved his life by a hair's breadth.

Coming back from the bridge barefoot, he trod on a snake. In a letter he himself explains to a friend, how in *Seven Pillars* the accident was told in a line and how he then filled four more "written with the finicky perfection of an armchair sitter, of the reflection of starlight on rocky ground. That's what I mean by perversity."

And why? Because he shies off the obvious and personal: his emotion, his fear when his life was in peril. And because he stresses "detached points, which a one-eyed man (or a man with his heart in the job) would not have seen".

During action, the looker-on wanted at all costs, to play as important a part as the actor. When it came to telling the story, the looker-on took the floor and emphasised the importance of his presence. But the actor who was watching him felt contempt for him and accused him of perverting, that is giving a garbled version of, the facts. We have first the critical spectator watching the actor and the scene of action, then the critical spectator describing the action and the scene, and finally the actor turned critic, slyly analysing the subtle twists which the critical spectator has given to the truth.

He is a critic at third degree.

> And thus the native hue of resolution
> Is sicklied o'er with the pale cast of thought
> And enterprises of great pitch and moment
> With this regard their currents turn awry
> And lose the name of action . . .*

It is the Hamlet side of Lawrence. Though, in him, did not paralyse the power of action, but disgusted him with it as a result of analysing it.

* *Hamlet.* III. i.

SCRUPLES AND AMBITIONS

THE CHAPTER OF *Seven Pillars* (No. CIII) in which he talks about himself, the key to the book, is full of contradictions, some purely on the surface, others fundamental.

His desire to please and his contempt for that feeling is most striking.

"Contempt for my passion for distinction made me refuse every offered honour."* Lawrence cherished his independence above all things; but he needed others in

---

* In *T. E. Lawrence by His Friends* Sir Winston Churchill relates how the author of *Seven Pillars* refused the order of Companion of the Bath in the middle of the ceremony, at the moment when the King was about to invest him with it, and how at a luncheon given in his house, he, Churchill, had reproached him for his behaviour, saying it was not fair on the King and there was no excuse for such a brutal and disrespectful action. To which Lawrence replied that it was the only way in his power of making the highest authorities realise that England's honour was compromised. An amusing footnote is : Churchill was mistaken as to what had taken place as Lawrence had refused the decoration at a private audience, before the investiture. But, as was his habit, Lawrence did not trouble to explain matters and smilingly accepted Churchill's reprimands. Churchill's admiration for Lawrence is expressed in the following words at the end of his contribution : "I deem him one of the greatest beings alive in our time. I do not see his like elsewhere, I fear that whatever our need we shall never see his like again."

order to get a picture of himself just as Narcissus
needed the brook to see his reflection. It was not, however, in order to admire himself that he wanted the
mirror, but in order to know what he was like for he
had little knowledge of himself. All that he knew were
the "bundled powers and entities" within himself, but
his central personality escaped him. He sought with
eager disquiet the stranger within himself whom he
feared, sought him in "the oblique overheard remarks
of others", in painted portraits and even in photographs. Lawrence was so afraid of meeting the unknown face to face that he only dared look at him side-
ways, or in front of a witness.

"The lower creation I avoided, as a reflection upon
our failure to attain real intellectuality." This is intel-
ligible in someone who believes in the influence of
example like Lawrence. But a few lines further on he
adds in a way which at first sight is disconcerting:

"I liked the things underneath me and took my
pleasures and adventures downward. There seemed a
certainty in degradation, a final safety."

This seems in flagrant disagreement with avoiding
lower creation. In reality I think it is a quite different
problem. Lawrence is seeking to be sure of something
in relation to his own personality. He is exploring. He
wants to find finality somewhere, firm bedrock. He had
found it once when he spent a fortnight coaling steam-
ers at Port Said. He found it again in after years work-

ing in the lowest rank in the Royal Air Force. Degradation here plays the part of the brook in which Narcissus saw himself. But why look for limits downwards? It was because he would find none on high. "Man could rise to any height, but there was an animal level beneath which he could not fall." I repeat this extraordinary aphorism. No hope of finding limits on high. In that case it would be impossible to find one's image by attempting to draw outlines where they retreat indefinitely, like the horizon.

In this definition of man, in this belief that man cannot fall below a certain level and that on the other hand he can rise to any height, Lawrence is giving a definition of himself. He is declaring his faith in man —and his declaration is based on transference and starts from an inner experience of his own. One thinks others guilty of a crime which one knows one is capable of oneself. One cannot have confidence in others unless one has confidence in oneself. One cannot have faith in man's goodness if one lacks "the milk of human kindness", or faith in his grandeur if one has always behaved meanly. This does not mean that you lack humility and modesty if you have a high opinion of the human race but that there is a touch of optimism in every worry about one's own moral cleanliness. It is a compensation for the sacrifices which have to be made if one is to acquire and to preserve it. Moral, like physical cleanliness is not acquired once and for all: it can only be kept and renewed by a habit of constant watchfulness and discipline.

Lawrence unable to measure the height to which he could reach wanted to ascertain the depths to which he could descend. A tree is bounded by the earth, if you examine the roots. The leaves stretch into an impalpable medium from which it draws its nourishment. Lawrence wished to study the earth-bound base of the tree because it was what was accessible.

He spoke of doubt as the modern crown of thorns. The only certainty was that man could not sink below a certain level. All else was thorny doubt. And that was why Lawrence chose the thorns after all. Though he boasted of liking degradation and of finding a finality in it, the attempt was doomed to failure because he could find no pleasure in it.

"I could see happiness in the supremacy of the material and could not surrender to it." Another certainty despised. But material happiness was only an apparent certainty. It can provide more or less ephemeral pleasures but not joy (in the Bergsonian sense of the word). The material has never made anyone shed tears of joy, whatever other satisfactions it may provide. With it happiness may be destroyed with a snap of the fingers by physical suffering. Whereas in the spiritual, as Lawrence knew, there is nothing incompatible between pain and joy.

"My brain was sudden and silent as a wild cat, my

senses like mud clogging its feet and myself (conscious always of itself and its shyness) telling the beast it was bad form to spring and vulgar to feed upon the kill."

To devour its prey is a law of nature for the animal. As for the brain, it was no doubt the prey which was thought vulgar and not feeding upon it. Only conscience can see that act from another point of view and give another interpretation. In Lawrence conscience mastered both his intelligence and his instincts. It could stand up to his will. And when Lawrence, speaking of *Seven Pillars,* says that "the book is the mangy skin of the animal inside him dried, stuffed and set up squarely for men to stare at" he is wrong. Not perhaps wrong as regards what he thinks he is presenting, but wrong about what the reader beholds.

VOLUNTARY SLAVERY

A MAN CRUCIFIED by his will and his will crucified by his conscience: that is what we are looking at. One can say of will power what Lawrence said of courage:

"It could not stand alone but must be mixed with a good or bad medium to appear." The author of *Seven Pillars* cultivated his will power for the love of it as he did his bodily muscles.

"When a desire gained head, I used to strive until I had just to open my hand and take it. Then I would turn away, content that it had been within my strength. I sought only to assure myself, and cared not a jot to make the others know it."

To satisfy his will he sought to measure his strength and to satisfy his pride he did not let the others know about it. Yet he was ready to put his powers at the service of those from whom he had concealed them. He said that as he could not approve of creative acts he would only serve and patch to make as good as could be what other men created. That is an extremely obscure statement. What did he mean by create? His ambition to write a book fit to put beside *The Brothers Karamazov, Thus Spake Zarathrustra* and *Moby Dick* was a purely creative ambition. Everything he says in this introspective chapter of *Seven Pillars* is as sincere as it is contradictory. But what seems to be least influenced by the sudden barometric changes of Fair to Stormy, of exaltation and despair, is Lawrence's thirst to serve a master, a thirst which his commanders did not understand. "They could not see that voluntary slavery was the deep pride of a morbid spirit, and vicarious pain its gladdest decoration."

Was he then incapable of commanding others with humility, since destiny had set him over other men? Was he impelled to serve proudly and to busy himself with subordinate jobs which perhaps other men would have done better, since they had been born to them? If command was more bitter than servitude why didn't his will force him to choose the thorny path? Why did he sweep the floor of a barracks when elsewhere there was no one to replace him? Did he not himself admit: "It's like having a unicorn in a racing stable. Beast doesn't fit."

Did the pleasure of seeing his will functioning like a powerful machine preoccupy him to such an extent that he finally failed to see that the slavery to which he submitted was no longer completely voluntary? Did Lawrence, that fanatic lover of freedom, become the slave of his fear of being enslaved? The mystics think that it is dangerous for those who would follow their way, to live in the external world and to take action before the inner world of contemplation has reached a certain stage. There is a risk of such acts proving evil in proportion as their doer's inner life is deficient.*

Had Lawrence entered the endless spiral of mystical requirements without being aware of it? Had he an intuitive knowledge of those esoteric truths which Bergson says are rather like music: you either hear it or you don't. And those who remain deaf to them cannot admit that they exist except in the fantasies of madmen who pretend to perceive them.

Perhaps he had suffered too much during his campaign in Arabia from the burden of authority and he trembled at the thought of it as his tortured body had trembled at Deraa at the threat of further wounds. Some of his experiences would by themselves have accounted for such a revulsion in a man like Lawrence. For instance the execution of Hamed which he describes with horror in *Seven Pillars*. It arose from an old blood-feud between two Arab clans. A corpse had been found. The guilty man was discovered. The family of the dead man claimed a life for a life according to Arab law in such circumstances. But if Hamed were killed by the family of the dead man endless reprisals would ensue which might end by jeopardising the unity of the Arab Revolt. Lawrence in despair, felt that there was only one solution: to take justice into his own hands because he was a neutral figure. To carry out the

* Aldous Huxley minutely analyses these problems in the pages he devotes to them in *Grey Eminence*.

execution himself in order to avoid the consequences.

"Then rose up the horror which would make civilised man shun justice like the plague if he had not the needy to serve him as hangmen for wages."

Lawrence killed Hamed. He was shaking so that his second bullet only broke the man's wrist. The chapter ends:

"They had to lift me into the saddle."

The responsibility of authority often leads to having to perform diabolical duties, particularly in the case of men who do not delegate their dirty work to others, and have not at their orders starving, or other damned souls to do it for them.

Bernard Shaw said:

"You must keep in mind that he was not like Haig or Allenby or Foch or Ludendorff giving orders and seeing little or nothing of their sanguinary effect. He had to do the most diabolical things with his own hands and see their atrocious results close up."

There was plenty to break the nerves of a man less sensitive and less imaginative than he was. Nor did he come out of such an existence unscathed.

RETIREMENT

A FTER HAVING LIVED through the events described in *Seven Pillars* Lawrence had to wear himself out in a conflict which was fought at Versailles, in Downing Street, and at Cairo. For three years he was forced to fight stubbornly for his views: the duty of keeping the promises made to the Arabs in the name of Great Britain. As he saw it the honour of his country was involved. To the bitterness of this long wrangle were added the physical effects of an aeroplane crash in which he sustained broken ribs and an injured lung. Together they left a greater mark upon him than all his battles with the Turks. One can understand the alternatives involved in this political battle from his letters.

"Do make clear to your lads"—he wrote in 1928 to an officer who had fought in Arabia—"that my objects were to save England and France too, from the follies of the imperialists, who would have us, n 1920, repeat the exploits of Clive or Rhodes. The world has passed by that point. I think, though, there's a great future for the British Empire as a voluntary association: and I'd like it to have Treaty States on a big scale attached to it. We've lots of Treaty States now, from Nepal downwards: let's have Egypt and Irak, at least, to add to them. We are so big a firm that we can offer unique advantages to smaller businesses to associate with us: if we can get out attractive terms of association."

Lawrence did not believe in racial superiority. He detested jingoism. In that as in everything else he seems to have been in complete opposition to Nazi doctrines. Formal discipline, for instance, seemed to him to solve problems in the wrong way. For soldiers it was a peace-time virtue.

Discipline "was not to impress upon men that their will must actively second the officer's, for then there would have been, as in the Arab army and among irregulars, that momentary pause for thought trans-mission, or digestion; for the nerves to resolve the relaying private will into active consequence. On the contrary, each regular Army sedulously rooted out this significant pause from its companies on parade. The drill-instructors tried to make obedience an instinct, a mental reflex, following as instantly on the command as though the motor power of the individual wills had been invested together in the system. This was well so far as it increased quickness: but it made no provision for casualties, beyond the weak assumption that each subordinate had his will-motor not atrophied, but reserved in perfect order, ready at the instant to take over his late superior's office...."

Lawrence did not believe it was. The feeling for formal discipline which results in saving a great deal of time carries with it the risk of paralysing everything in the individual except his mechanical reflexes. That is a serious disadvantage. And if the same sort of discipline applies to all orders given to the public in a country, the dangers grow proportionally greater. That is what happens in totalitarian states.

Yet—and here is another example of the contradictions in this tormented spirit—Lawrence shut himself up within the precincts of formal discipline for the last years of his life, from 1922 to 1935. Refusing to accept any post corresponding to the merit of his achievements, or his fame, Lawrence crept away under an assumed name—his own would have made such action impossible—as an ordinary airman in the R.A.F., then as a private in the Royal Tank Corps, then again as an airman. He felt a prisoner of the name he bore and which he had done everything to make famous at a time when he was dazzled by the thought of glory: the name which is now qualified by the words "of Arabia".

> Nor I, nor any man, that but man is,
> With nothing shall be pleas'd, till he be eas'd
> With being nothing.*

He had reached the point of preferring being nothing: of calling himself Shaw or Ross and not Lawrence of Arabia. His ideal, no doubt, would have been to have had no more than the perfectly reassuring anonymity

* Shakespeare. *Richard II*, v. v.

of a number. In 1930 his number in the R.A.F. was 338171. His friends naturally knew about his game of hide and seek and of his hiding place. Noël Coward wrote to him:

"Dear 338171, may I call you 338?"

Lawrence who loved a joke thought this one so good that he showed the letter to everyone. He himself had a great sense of humour. His letters are full of wit and the most mischievous inconsequences delighted him. He amused himself like a street arab.

HUMOUR

IN SPITE OF a pervading seriousness of tone, *Seven Pillars* sparkles with gleams of humour. It shows itself everywhere impishly: in the description of that crazy evening when the music of the Turkish band died away in a flabby discord of drums (the parchment of the drumheads had stretched in the damp air) while the Sherif of Mecca listened over the telephone to its rendering of "Deutschland über Alles"; in the relentless hospitality of Sheikh Fahad-el-Hansha urging his guest to a verminous seat and making him drink bowl after bowl of camel's milk (a powerful diuretic) while he assailed him with questions about the camel pastures of England: in the story of the Arab chieftain who left the banquet to smash his Turkish false teeth upon a rock and swore that henceforward he would only eat with an Allied set.

At every moment this humour enters even into the most dramatic events. It corresponds to Lawrence's grin which all his friends knew so well. When his publisher sent him a number of queries about the proofs of *Revolt in the Desert* he replied with the mockery and contempt which always rose to the surface when he came across people who took things too seriously.

They pointed out that Jedha, the she-camel, was spelled Jedhah on slip 40. He replied: "She was a splendid beast." They asked him whether he had written "Meleager the immoral poet". They had corrected it to "immortal". He replied: "Immorality I know. Immortality I cannot judge. As you please. Meleager will not sue us for libel." They pointed out that the Arabs called him "Ya-Aurans" and also "Aurans". Lawrence replied: "Also Lurens and Runs: not to mention Shaw. More to follow if time permits." He was told that the critics would take exception to his oddities of spelling of Arab proper names. So much the worse. "Arabic names won't go in English exactly for the consonants are not the same as ours and their vowels, like ours, vary from district to district. There are 'scientific systems' of transliteration, helpful to people who know enough Arabic not to need helping, but a wash-out for the world. I spell my names anyhow to show what rot the systems are."

Lawrence had never been respectful to systems and conventions.

LAST YEARS

DURING THE YEARS of his retirement in the R.A.F. and in the Royal Tank Corps, which lasted from 1922 until March 1935, he did other work besides scrubbing floors and such drudgery. He found time to translate the *Odyssey,* to help treble the speed of the R.A.F. air-sea rescue boats and other marine craft, and to write *The Mint.**

The Mint tells the story of life in barracks. Lawrence said that the descriptions were written not with his brain but with his senses. They are more pitilessly crude and stark than anything in the pages of *Seven Pillars.* After reading *The Mint* David Garnett wrote to his author:

"The Damascus hospital is sweet with the smell of flowers compared with the corroding breath of servitude: the cowardice of being bullied, and waiting for the insulting order . . ."

* His retirement took him to India, where he was sent in December 1926. He remained there until February 1929, first at Karachi, and then at Miranshah. He did not leave camp there and saw nothing of the country, as is shown by many letters written at this time. He employed his leisure hours in translating Homer. In the midst of this the London press published articles on his imaginary activities in Afghanistan—they said he was assisting the rebels—the press drew attention to him, revealed his identity and he had to return to England.

It was in that environment that Lawrence had chosen to live. It is necessary to point out that the atmosphere of the R.A.F. and that of the Royal Tank Corps seemed very different to him. In the R.A.F. the men were settled in a profession which they really cared about. They spoke eagerly of their work and of their future. Whereas the men in the Tank Corps had joined it because they were no good anywhere else. They had no interest in the Army or in their work, but only in the money it earned them and in the food they ate. In the Tank Corps the officers felt superior to the men and behaved accordingly. In the R.A.F. officers and men felt an underlying equality.

In March 1935, eight weeks before his death, Lawrence went to live in his little cottage in Dorset, Clouds Hill. There were two rooms, books, and gramophone records. His passion for reading and for music had never failed. Bernard Shaw assures us that Lawrence had a "perfectly ridiculous adoration of literature and authors".

His criticism of books was always acute. Of modern poets he said: "Poets of today feel often that their real feelings are foolish. So they splash something about shirt-sleeves or oysters quickly into every sentimental sentence, to prevent us laughing at them before they have laughed at themselves."

In spite of literature and music in his beloved Clouds Hill, Lawrence felt as he expressed it to Kennington:

"Have you ever been a leaf and fallen from your tree in autumn and been really puzzled about it? That's the feeling."

Winston Churchill did not intend to leave him long in this retirement. There was already a question—though nothing definite had been settled—of entrusting him with the reorganisation of Home Defence. Would he have ended by accepting it? He was afraid of his power of influencing people and through them, the course of events, for, after reflection, his ideas, or the work he could put them to, seemed to him second-hand. He asked himself if his convictions were not rationalisations, born of his wish to provide motives for exercising his powers. The notion filled him with such disgust that he wished to cut out all possibility of using power.

That was what he had sought when he enlisted in the ranks. He wanted to prevent the possibility of anyone thinking of him for a responsible position.

"Self-degradation is my aim."

When he gave way in a letter to violent expression of disgust for the men among whom he was living, he repented of it, apologised for it, and said that perhaps with time he would be able to repeat, thinking of them, the astonishing cry of Blake: "Everything that is, is holy." Then he added: "But not many other reflective men come to the same conclusion without a web of mysticism to help them."

THE END

ON THE 13TH of May he got on his motorcycle to send a telegram from Bovington Camp post office. This motorcycle had a name, like all those he had owned. They were precious, almost living things in his eyes. There had been a whole series of Georges, the last of which, George VIII, was being specially built for him at that time and was never delivered.

Lawrence took speed as some men take drugs. When he was almost ill with the life he led shut up in barracks, he found that a run of several hours through the country restored him. At high speeds he felt that he escaped from everything—even from the body. If the road were empty he would travel insanely fast. But he was always careful not to endanger anyone else's life by his recklessness.

On the 13th of May, returning to Clouds Hill, he swerved violently to avoid hitting two cyclists who were unexpectedly in his way, lost control and was flung off his motorcycle.

He had been thrown once over the head of his camel in the middle of battle. But on this occasion he could not repeat some lines brought up from adolescent

memory, as he had done when he felt himself lost in
the middle of the enemy.

> For Lord I was free of all Thy flowers,
> But I chose the world's sad roses
> And that is why my feet are torn
> And mine eyes are blind with sweat.

There was no enemy and it was a peaceful English
country road. Lawrence's brain and sight were destroyed. His body survived, unconscious, for five days.

Had he time in which to see his danger? Was he
aware of his end? Of the irony of things? That he
should die thus in an ordinary road accident owing to
two inoffensive cyclists, after having braved so many
dangers, survived so many perils, air crashes, bombings,
battles; tormented by thirst, fever, cold and burning
sun, blows, infected wounds, bones broken and badly
set.

Did Lawrence have that flash in which one can see
the whole of one's life which, they say, precedes sudden
death? Looking back did he pity himself as on that day
when he found his friend Hogarth and poured out his
bitterness and disappointments? The day on which he
said that he was tired:

"I was tired to death of free-will, and of many things
besides free-will. For a year and a half I had been in
motion, riding a thousand miles a month upon camels:
with added nervous hours in crazy aeroplanes, or rush-

ing across country in powerful cars. In my last five actions I had been hit, and my body so dreaded further pain that now I had to force myself under fire. Generally I had been hungry: lately always cold: and frost and dirt had poisoned my hurts into a festering mass of sores.

"However, these worries would have taken their due petty place, in my despite of the body, and of my soiled body in particular, but for the rankling fraudulence which had to be my mind's habit."

And also he was afraid.

". . . I feared to be alone lest the winds of circumstance, or power or lust, blow my empty soul away."

Fear of the communion of that body whose appetites he despised and of his aimless soul which refused to admit to its own emptiness. Fear of the mystery of the inadmissible void, fear of the eternal silence of infinite space watched over by the jealous stars, fear of those silent witnesses before whom he had once boasted:

"and wrote my will across the sky in stars."

Fear that their constellations should betray what he had hidden from himself: an appetite baulked of love, to which every form of self-denial had become essential, for which every ordeal had become fruitful. A thirst for the ultimate that no one in the least human could assuage, neither victories in arms, nor those in the arts, nor satiated ambition, nor the satisfaction of disdaining the pride which had brought them to birth. A thirst for the ultimate which could only be quenched in the inevitable failure in which every triumph founders; in which every goal reached is not a glorious arrival but a new point of departure. A departure in search of who knows what spoils and conquests for which the need and the chase are even more incomprehensible for those deprived of faith than the eternal silence of infinite space before which faith itself trembles and recoils.

Mar del Plata–San Isidro
May–June 1942